Dedication

This book is dedicated to you, the reader and user of this manual. May it be instrumental in broadening your knowledge of seafood, and may it bring a new and exciting dimension to your lifestyle . . . Enjoy!

Contents

Preface

Bill and I can hardly believe this book is to become a reality. Over the last several years it's been added to, subtracted from, nearly forgotten, the center of dreams. It is more than a cookbook to us, it's a collection of stories and memories, a culinary record of our married life.

I came to the coast with my parents in 1962. My father had been offered a job in the oyster business, so we packed our belongings, left the cold regions of northern Minnesota, and moved to the beautiful little town of Poulsbo, "Little Norway," on Washington's Puget Sound.

So began my family's enthusiasm for seafoods, and for exploring the seafood world. Within a few years my father had opened three fish markets from Bainbridge Island to Bremerton, and was handling everything from ling cod to live lobsters. As I worked in these markets I learned about the qualities of seafoods, and the special care required to prolong their freshness and delicate flavors.

I also learned to my amazement that, although most of our customers lived beside the sea, they had very limited ideas about how to prepare seafoods.

They wanted to know what to do with all those goodies, and they were asking me! Being an experimental cook anyway, I accepted the challenge willingly, and soon I found other experimental cooks who were willing to share their ideas with me. As my familiarity with seafoods grew, so did my desire to share what I learned.

It was while I was working for my father that I met my husband, Bill, and we discovered a common interest in cooking and eating. (I still believe it was the crab-stuffed scampi that hooked him!) Bill, native to the Pacific Northwest, is a skilled outdoorsman with vast expertise in fishing and hunting. He also loves to cook, and we've had a wonderful time rounding out our knowledge of seafoods together.

After years of experimenting with seafoods and talking to people about how to prepare them, Bill encouraged me to write down our hodgepodge of recipes and gather our favorites into the collection presented here. We hope you'll enjoy them. Use them as they are, then as a point of departure for your own imagination. With very little effort and expense, you can create your own masterpieces to share.

Introduction

How To Select Seafoods

You can rely on all of your senses to select quality seafoods.

All seafoods should be visually appealing (color being the primary concern here), they should be clean and free of slimy residue to touch, and free of unpleasant (ammoniated or fishy) odors.

In the case of pre-cooked seafoods, ask for a sample to taste. Whether or not you have had excellent quality seafoods before, the taste test will tell you immediately if this is a product that appeals to you and one that you will want to purchase.

You can even use your sense of hearing to select high grade seafoods. Listen to others who have shopped for seafoods before. They will let you know what market will give you the quality you're looking for. Care should be given in selecting your market since proper handling of seafood is so critical in assuring freshness.

The following check-points will help you make the best possible selections.

When purchasing

Fresh Whole Fish

- ✓ __the eyes__ – they should be clear, bright and full. (As fish get old, the eyes become cloudy and shrink.)
- ✓ __the gills__ – they should be bright red and free of slime. (As fish get old, the gills fade to a light pink, then gray and even brown.)
- ✓ __the skin__ – it should be shiny with distinct color that has not faded.
- ✓ __the flesh__ – it should be firm and elastic and tight against the bones.

Fresh Fish Fillets or Steaks

- ✓ __the flesh__ – it should be fresh-cut in appearance with color that resembles freshly-dressed fish. (As fish gets old, the flesh color fades and becomes soft and slimy.)

When purchasing

Frozen Fish

✓ <u>the flesh</u> - it should be
frozen solid, have no
discoloration, white cottony
appearance or brownish
tinge.
✓ <u>for odor</u> - it should have a
very slight odor or no odor
at all.
✓ <u>the packaging</u> - it should be
air-tight.
✓ <u>for ice glazing</u> - in some
cases, this method is used
to protect against drying out.

Fresh Clams and Oysters in the Shell

✓ <u>for life</u> - if they are alive
their shells will close tightly
when their position is disturbed.

Shucked Oysters

✓ <u>the color</u> - they should have a
natural creamy color with
a dark brown to black skirt.
✓ <u>the liquid</u> - they should have
a minimum amount of clear,
slightly opalescent liquid.
✓ <u>for odor</u> - they should have a
mild, non-offensive odor.

When purchasing

Cooked Crabs and Lobsters

✓ *the color* - they should be bright red-orange and free of greenish slime.
✓ *for odor* - they should have a mild, agreeable odor (As crabs and lobsters get old, they take on a strong, ammoniated odor.)

Fresh Shrimp

✓ *the meat* - it should be firm in texture
✓ *for odor* - presence of an ammoniated odor means the shrimp are old. Fresh shrimp will have a mild odor.

Cooked Shrimp

✓ *the color* - the shells should be pink to dark orange to red. The meat should have a reddish tint and may have darker red spots.
✓ *for odor* - they should have a mild, agreeable odor.

When purchasing

Scallops

✓ <u>the meat</u> - it should be firm
in texture and free of excess
liquid, but not to the point
of being dry.
✓ <u>for odor</u> - scallops have a
sweetish odor when fresh.

Always check with the salesperson
to see if the seafood you are
purchasing has been frozen and
thawed. If so, <u>do not re-freeze it</u>.

Nutritional Values

Seafood is a rich source of protein, minerals and vitamins. People of all ages can use fish and shellfish to provide a high quality diet. Here is how seafood rates in the principal nutritive values:

<u>Protein</u> : An excellent source of very good and easily digestible protein. A four ounce serving of fish will provide about one third of an adult's daily protein requirement. To balance incomplete cereal and vegetable proteins, nutritionists recommend that about one third of daily protein come from animal sources. Fish or shellfish will meet this need.

<u>Vitamins</u>: Fat fish such as salmon, black cod, tuna, mackerel and herring are rich in vitamins A and D. All fish oils are rich in vitamin D. Both fat and lean fish contain some of the B vitamins. Overall, fish contribute generously to the body's vitamin needs.

<u>Minerals</u>: Minerals found in generous amounts in fish and shellfish include copper, iron, magnesium and phosphorous and in some fish, calcium. In general, the mineral content of fish is similar to that of beef. However, fish provides more iodine and other needed trace minerals

such as cobalt and zinc. Saltwater fish and shellfish, in fact, contain more iodine than any other food. They are also more easily digested than beef.

Fish and shellfish, as with other foods, will offer more food value if used when fresh. Proper storage and various cooking methods will be a determining factor in nutritional wealth.

Red Tide & Shellfish

There are several natural conditions that can create a red tide, but only one of these conditions produces toxicity levels harmful to people who eat affected shellfish.

A toxic condition is created by the presence of Gonyaulax, a microscopic red-celled organism that has a paralyzing affect on mammals, including humans.

These organisms develop during the summer months (any time between April and October), when shellfish are normally in their worst condition anyway, and when water temperatures are warmer.

This form of contaminant is almost exclusively confined to high salinity waters off the Pacific Coast and the Strait of Juan de Fuca. Although red tide conditions exist in the Puget Sound, the Gonyaulax infection is rare in this area. It is extremely important, however, to heed all warnings regarding red tide areas issued by the health and fisheries departments.

Gonyaulax usually affects the meat of clams, oysters and mussels for about six weeks after the red tide bloom. Butter clams, however, can retain the toxicity for up to 24 months.

Most of the toxic elements are concentrated in the black tip of the siphon and gills of clams. To reduce the possibilities of toxic reactions and increase your margin of safety, cut away and discard these sections before cooking. You may want to make this a common practice, not only during the summer months when red tide conditions exist, but throughout the year.

Tips for Freezing

Fish : When freezing fish, dip in icy cold water. Lay steaks or fillets in a single layer on a flat surface. A cookie sheet works very well. Freeze solid. Remove fish and dip in ice water again. When frozen solid, remove from tray and place in plastic bags. This glazing process will protect your fish from freezer burn and lock in freshness without drowning out the fine fish flavor. This process of individual quick-freezing also works well for roasts and whole fish. Remember, to avoid loss of moisture, don't thaw fish fully before you start to cook it.

Oysters : The individual quick-freezing method may be used for oysters as well. It isn't necessary to dip oysters in ice water a second time. You may wish to prepare oysters for pan frying (see Pan fried Oysters) before freezing. Freeze individually on a flat surface, place in plastic bags, then simply remove as many oysters as you require and they are ready to go - from freezer to frying pan.

Remember to date your frozen foods, rotate your stock and try to use items within two to four weeks after freezing to insure full flavor and higher nutritional value.

Shellfish

Basically, shellfish are divided into two classifications. The first group are called crustaceans. These include crab, lobster and shrimp. The second group, referring to the muscles, are called mollusks. Mollusks with hard outer shells include oysters, clams, scallops and mussels. Mollusks without hard outer shells are the octopus and the squid.

Shellfish are among the most delicate and perishable of all foods. Avoid "bargains" unless you are sure of top quality. Purchase only the best quality shellfish - these are not necessarily the most expensive. Because they are so perishable, shellfish should be refrigerated until you are ready to use them. They also need to be used as quickly as possible (within one or two days after purchasing). Remember these two important tips to be assured of the finest flavor and texture and the best nutritional value.

Crabs

Although there are many varieties of this crustacean, the most common are the Blue Crab of Chesapeake Bay and the Atlantic and Gulf coasts, the Dungeness Crab of the Pacific Coast and the Alaskan King Crab. Any one of these varieties may be used in recipes calling for crabmeat.

Crab may be purchased live, cooked in the shell, fresh or frozen or canned. Cooked crab in the shell should be bright red and free of any disagreeable odor. A very perishable food, fresh or frozen crab is best when used within one or two days after purchasing. To avoid spoiling, it should be kept on ice or refrigerated until you are ready to use it.

The following recipes will help you discover the elegant simplicity of serving this most popular seafood.

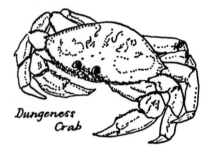

Dungeness
Crab

To cook live crabs : Use ¼ cup salt per quart of fresh water. Bring to a boil and drop crabs into the boiling water upside down. The crabs will fold their legs against their shells and die instantly. Cover and boil for 20 minutes. Cool quickly in cold water. When cool, clean and crack for use immediately or freeze whole for use later.

To clean whole crabs : Under cold running water pull off back and remove viscera and gills. Rinse out yellow fat. Scrub back and freeze in plastic bag for future use in Crab Thermidor or Crab Louis.

To crack crab : Pull off legs singly, starting from small legs. Break body in half and pick meat from each half using a small, sharp object. A nutpick works great! Next, crack legs slightly on joints and on edges. A nutcracker or small hammer will do nicely. Leg meat is then easily removed intact. The leg pieces are nice toppers for that extra-special crab cocktail or excellent for sautéing.

Sautéed Crab Legs

1 clove garlic, minced
3 Jblsp. butter
1 Jblsp. fresh snipped
   parsley
⅛ tsp. lemon pepper

10-12 large crab
   legs, shelled
¼ cup dry white
   wine

Melt butter in saucepan over low heat. Add garlic, parsley and lemon pepper. Simmer for 1 minute. Gently add crab legs. Sauté for 1-2 minutes on each side. Slowly add wine. Sauté 2 minutes longer. Remove to heated chafing dish. Serve immediately. A super hors d'oeuvre with a dash extraordinaire! Serves 4-6.

Crab Custard

1 lb. crabmeat
2 Tblsp. melted butter
4 slices white bread,
    trimmed
1 cup grated cheese
2 Tblsp. parsley
2 Tblsp. minced onion

3 cups milk
4 eggs, well beaten
½ tsp. salt
¼ tsp. white pepper *
1 tsp. Worcestershire
paprika

Pour butter in 8 x 8 x 2 baking pan. Place bread in a single layer in bottom of baking pan. Arrange crabmeat over bread. Sprinkle cheese, parsley and onion over crabmeat. Combine milk, eggs, salt, pepper and Worcestershire; pour over crab. Top with paprika. Set baking dish in a larger pan containing 1 inch of hot water. Bake at 350°F. for 45-50 minutes or until knife inserted in the center comes out clean. Serves 4-6.

* <u>White Pepper</u> :   crack whole peppercorns; discard outer black shell. Grind white core.

Crab Roll-ups

2 lbs. fresh fillet of sole (fairly thick and large)
½ lb. fresh crab meat   ¼ tsp. lemon pepper
¼ cup celery, diced small   ½ cup dry white wine
⅛ cup bread crumbs   sour cream
¼ cup butter   fresh snipped parsley

Sprinkle fillets with lemon pepper and refrigerate. Combine crab meat, celery, bread crumbs and half of butter. Place 1 or 2 tablespoons of the mixture in the center of each fillet and roll, being careful to keep mixture in the center. Fasten with wooden picks or skewers. Place fillets in baking dish, cover with wine and dot with remaining butter. Cover and bake at 350°F. for 20-30 minutes or until fish flakes easily with a fork. Top each roll-up with a dab of sour cream. Return to oven for 3 minutes. Garnish with parsley. Serves 4-6.

Crab Cakes with Mornay Sauce

2 eggs, slightly beaten
2 Tblsp. mayonnaise
1 tsp. Dijon mustard
1 tsp. seafood seasoning
cooking oil for frying

1 tsp. parsley flakes
3 cups soft bread
 crumbs
2⅔ cups fresh crab-
 meat

Combine egg, mayonnaise, mustard, seafood seasoning and parsley. Stir in bread crumbs and crabmeat. Shape into 6-8 patties. (Make more by making them smaller if you plan to use them as hors d'oeuvres.) In a skillet, brown patties in a little hot oil over medium heat 3-4 minutes, turning once. Serve hot with Mornay Sauce (see SAUCES). Serves 4-6.

Crab Stuffed Scampi

2 lbs. large Scampi
½ lb. crab meat
¼ cup bread crumbs
½ cup melted butter

seafood seasoning
parsley flakes
lemon wedges

Combine crab meat, bread crumbs, ¼ cup butter and seafood seasoning to taste. Refrigerate while you prepare prawns. Leave Scampi in the shell. Slice down underside of Scampi removing tiny feelers. Devein. Season lightly with seafood seasoning. Stuff each with crab meat mixture. Place in baking dish; drizzle remaining butter on top. Sprinkle with parsley. Bake at 350°F. for 10-15 minutes or until Scampi turns white. Remove to serving platter and garnish with lemon wedges. Serves 4-6.

Crab Thermidor

2 lbs. cooked crabmeat
½ cup chopped mushrooms
1 small green pepper,
 chopped fine
3 green onions, minced
2 tomatoes, peeled and
 chopped
3 Tblsp. butter
1 cup cream

2 Tblsp. fresh
 snipped parsley
salt and pepper
½ cup buttered
 bread crumbs
lemon wedges
fresh parsley
 sprigs

Combine crab with mushrooms, green pepper, onions and tomatoes. Cook in butter for 10 minutes; add cream and simmer for 5 minutes longer. Add parsley, salt and pepper. Fill washed crab shells or individual baking dishes with mixture, cover with buttered bread crumbs and brown in 350°F. oven. Garnish with lemon wedges and parsley sprigs. Serves 6-8.

Avocado Crabmeat Cocktail

½ cup Cocktail Sauce (see SAUCES)
¼ cup mayonnaise   1 tsp. fresh snipped parsley
¼ cup cooking sherry   ½ lb. fresh crabmeat
1 tsp. lemon juice   1 cup diced, ripe avocado
dash cayenne   ½ cup celery, diced fine

Reserve 4 or more of the larger crab leg pieces to garnish cocktails. Mix together cocktail sauce, mayonnaise, sherry, lemon juice, cayenne and parsley. Cover and chill 1 hour or more. Shortly before serving, mix cocktail sauce mixture with crabmeat, avocado and celery. Serve in individual cocktail glasses. Garnish with reserved crab leg pieces.

NOTE: Lobster, shrimp or flaked white fish may be substituted for the crabmeat.

Crab Quiche

1/4 lb. bacon	1/2 tsp. salt
1/2 cup onion, chopped fine	dash cayenne
1/2 lb. swiss cheese, grated	dash nutmeg
3 eggs, slightly beaten	1/2 lb. crabmeat
2 cups half and half or cream	Plain Pastry *

Cook bacon until crisp; crumble and set aside. Reserve 1 Tblsp. of the bacon drippings. Cook onion in reserved bacon fat until golden. Line a 9" pie pan with pastry and bake for 5 minutes at 450°F. Remove from the oven and sprinkle with bacon and onion. Cover with grated cheese. Mix together eggs, cream, salt, cayenne and nutmeg. Pour into pie shell. Add crabmeat. Bake 10 minutes and reduce heat to 325°F.; bake until firm (about 30 minutes). Cut in pie-shaped wedges and serve with a dollup of sour cream and a dash of tobasco if you wish. Serves 6.

* Plain Pastry

1 cup flour	dash salt
1/3 cup plus 1 Tblsp. shortening	1/4 cup cold water

Combine flour and salt. Cut in shortening with pastry cutter or fork. Blend until mixture forms small balls about the size of peas. Add water, shape into ball and roll out on floured board. Makes pastry to line 1-9" pan.

Crab Cutlets

3 Tblsp. butter
3 Tblsp. flour
1½ cups milk
salt and pepper to taste
1 egg, slightly beaten
dash celery salt

2 tsp. grated onion
2 cups crabmeat
mayonnaise
dry bread crumbs
3 Tblsp. butter
lemon wedges

Melt 3 Tblsp. butter; blend in flour. Add milk and cook, stirring constantly, until thick and creamy. Remove from heat; stir in salt and pepper, egg, celery salt, grated onion and crabmeat. Chill for several hours. Form into cakes or cut into triangular shapes. Dip each into flour, spread generously on both sides with mayonnaise and roll in crumbs. Brown in the remaining 3 Tblsp. butter and serve with Cheese Sauce (see SAUCES) and lemon wedges. Serves 6.

Lobster

Lobster is a favorite food delicacy because of its rich, flavorful meat and also because of the attractive ways of serving afforded to the imaginative cook. Not only do lobsters lend eye-appeal to your menu, they are also rich in energy-giving glycogen; the reason for their sweet flavor.

Although lobsters are in season all year, they are most plentiful during the summer months when more lobsters are closer to shores.

Whole lobster may be bought live, or you may purchase the tails frozen. Very large lobsters tend to have a coarser texture than the medium and smaller varieties. For those special cocktails and salads, canned lobster meat is also available.

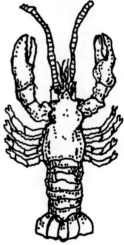

Lobster Thermidor

2 lbs. cooked lobster meat
⅓ cup chopped mushrooms
1 small green pepper,
   chopped fine
2 pimiento, chopped fine
3 green onions, minced
½ cup buttered bread
   crumbs

2 tomatoes, peeled
   and chopped
3 Tblsp. butter
1 cup cream
2 Tblsp. fresh parsley,
   chopped
salt and pepper
   to taste

Combine lobster with mushrooms, green pepper, pimiento, green onions and tomatoes. Simmer in butter for 10 minutes. Add cream and continue cooking for 5 minutes, stirring constantly. Remove from heat; add parsley, salt and pepper. Fill washed lobster shells or individual oven-proof dishes with mixture. Cover with buttered crumbs and brown in 350°F. oven. Garnish with lemon wedges. Serves 6-8.

Lobster Cocktail

Allow 2 cups shredded fresh cooked or canned lobster meat for 6 servings. Arrange in cocktail glasses and top with Cocktail Sauce (see SAUCES) and a sprinkle of parsley. Garnish with lemon wedges, a small sprig of fresh parsley and a slice of hard-boiled egg. Very attractive served in small, clear glass bowls inside larger clear glass bowls partially filled with crushed ice.

Broiled Lobster

4 large lobster tails, thawed
5-6 quarts water
1 tsp. salt
lemon pepper

Bouquet Garni –
(see page 34)
4 Tblsp. butter

Bring water to a boil. Add salt and Bouquet Garni. Boil 3-5 minutes. Remove Bouquet Garni and add lobster tails. Boil 10-15 minutes or until meat turns white. Drain. Slit tails down soft side of shell with shears or sharp knife. Peel back shell to expose meat. Top each with 1 Tblsp. butter and sprinkle with lemon pepper. Place in baking dish and broil 2-3 minutes. Serve with melted butter, salad and French rolls. Serves 4.

Grilled Lobster-Stuffed Mushrooms

24 large mushrooms
¼ cup chopped green onions
1 Tblsp. butter
2 tsp. flour
½ tsp. dried marjoram, crushed
dash pepper
¼ cup dry white wine

½ cup cooked lobster, finely chopped
1 Tblsp. fresh parsley, snipped
2 Tblsp. butter
⅓ cup bread crumbs
1 Tblsp. lemon juice

Remove stems from mushrooms; reserve caps. Chop stems. In medium saucepan, sauté chopped stems and onion in 1 Tblsp. butter until tender. Blend in flour, marjoram and pepper. Add wine. Cook and stir until thickened and bubbly. Stir in lobster and parsley. Stuff mushroom caps with lobster mixture. Place mushrooms on a large piece of foil; dot with remaining butter, sprinkle with bread crumbs and lemon juice. Fold foil to seal edges. Grill over medium coals 15-20 minutes or until mushrooms are tender. You may also bake in oven at 300°F. instead of grilling, or broil 5 minutes if you prefer the mushrooms less cooked. Makes 24 appetizers.

NOTE: To clean commercial mushrooms quickly and thoroughly, place in plastic bag with 1 cup cold water and 2 Tblsp. lemon juice. Shake vigorously until mushrooms look creamy white. Drain and rinse with cold water.

Shrimp

When fresh, shrimp have a mild odor and the meat is firm in texture. Their shells range in color from grayish-green to pinkish-tan to light pink, depending on the species and where it is caught.

When shrimp are cooked, their shells turn a bright red and the meat takes on similar appealing reddish tints, occasionally with some dark red spots.

The term 'shrimp' refers to the tail section of the shrimp, fresh, frozen or cooked. Prawns are large shrimp, usually the jumbo gulf-area shrimp.

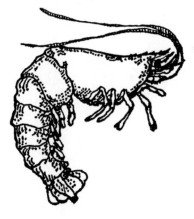

Shrimp Club Sandwich

2 Tblsp. butter
2 Tblsp. flour
½ tsp. seafood
   seasoning
dash cayenne
1 cup canned milk

1 cup water
2 cups tiny Pacific
   shrimp
¾ cup grated cheese
sliced tomatoes
buttered toast points

Melt butter in pan. Add flour and seasonings. Stir until well blended. Add milk and water, stirring constantly until smooth and creamy (about 10 minutes). Add shrimp and heat through. Spoon over buttered toast points and sprinkle with grated cheese. Put tomato slices on top and place under broiler until cheese is melted and tomato is slightly cooked. Serves 4.

Shrimp Boats Is a Comin'

1 large, ripe pineapple
1-8oz. pkg. cream cheese
½ lb. tiny Pacific shrimp, drained
⅓ cup mayonnaise
2 tsp. lemon juice
⅓ cup grated cheese

⅔ cup chopped walnuts
2 Tblsp. fresh snipped parsley
sour cream
brown sugar

Soften cream cheese. Cut pineapple in half lengthwise, leaving the green top on. Remove core down center and discard. Remove fruit by cutting around pineapple about ½" from outer skin. Cut into large triangular-shaped pieces. Refrigerate. To softened cream cheese, add mayonnaise and lemon juice. Blend well. Add shrimp and grated cheese and form into small balls. Roll in chopped nuts and parsley and refrigerate for 2 hours. Remove from refrigerator ½ hour before serving. To serve, pierce pineapple chunks and shrimp balls with picks. Pile into pineapple shells. Serve with sour cream and brown sugar condiments to dip pineapple chunks in, if you like. A beautiful addition to anyone's table. Perfect for that special barbecue or buffet luncheon.

Orient Express

1 lb. large raw shrimp
¼ lb. fresh mushrooms, sliced
¼ cup green pepper, chopped
1 small sweet red pepper, sliced
¼ cup chopped onion
2 medium tomatoes, peeled and sliced in wedges

dash lemon pepper
dash ground ginger
2 Tblsp. butter
¼ tsp. salt
1 pkg. frozen Chinese peapods
1 small can tomato sauce
2 Tblsp. flour
½ cup cold water
1 Tblsp. soy sauce

Shell and devein shrimp. Butterfly if very large. In saucepan, melt butter; add mushrooms, green pepper, red pepper, onion, tomatoes and peapods. Sauté about 3 minutes. Add shrimp and cook until shrimp is light pink in color and vegetables are tender. Season with lemon pepper, salt and ginger. Stir in tomato sauce. Shake 2 Tblsp. flour in cold water and add to mixture. Add soy sauce. Cook, stirring constantly, until thickened. Serve in center of rice ring and garnish with fresh parsley sprigs. Serves 4.

Rice Ring

Pack hot, cooked white rice into
well buttered ring mold. Let stand
a few minutes then unmold on a
serving platter. Fill with shrimp and
vegetable combination such as Orient
Express, or create your own seafood
combo to serve in this attractive mold.

Hot Creamy Shrimp Dip

1 8oz. pkg. cream cheese
1 ½ cups tiny Pacific
  shrimp (reserve juice)
1 tsp. lemon juice
⅓ cup chopped black
  olives

½ pkg. dry onion
  soup
¼ cup milk
3 Tblsp. fresh-
  snipped parsley

Blend softened cream cheese, milk,
onion soup, lemon juice, parsley and
reserved juice from shrimp in blender
until smooth. Pour into saucepan, add
shrimp and black olives. Stir constantly
over low heat until hot. Serve with
fresh vegetables, crackers or your
favorite chips. You may substitute
crabmeat for the shrimp if you like.

Boiled Prawns

2 qts. water
3 lbs. prawns in the
   shell (raw)

Bouquet Garni *

Bring water to a boil ; add Bouquet Garni. Reduce heat and simmer 5 minutes. Rinse prawns in ice cold water. Add to boiling water. Cook about 3 minutes or just until prawns turn deep pink. <u>Do not overcook</u>. Shell, devein and add to Creole Sauce to serve over hot cooked rice, or serve "shell 'em yourself" style with Creole Sauce as a condiment. (see SAUCES.)

* Bouquet Garni

whole thyme
whole marjoram
peppercorn

2 cloves garlic
parsley sprigs

Use a 3"x3" square of cheesecloth. Put equal amounts of ingredients in center of cheesecloth. Draw corners together and close top with string.

Beer-Boiled Shrimp

2 qts. water
2 bay leaves
1 Tblsp. salt

5 lbs. raw shrimp
1 small can beer

Add bay leaves and salt to water and bring to a full boil. Add beer and shrimp and cook until shrimp turn a deep pink (about 3-5 minutes). Drain, shell and devein. Serve with Thousand Island Dressing, Cocktail Sauce, Creole Sauce or Lemon-Dill Mayonnaise (see SAUCES). Serves 8-10.

Shrimp Muffins Delight

2 7½ oz. cans tiny
    Pacific shrimp
¼ cup chopped black
    olives
1 medium tomato,
    chopped
½ tsp. seafood
    seasoning
4 small green onions,
    chopped fine

4 English muffins,
    split
½ tsp. lemon juice
1 tsp. fresh-snipped
    parsley
¼ cup mayonnaise
8 slices Monterey
    Jack cheese

Combine shrimp, black olives, tomato,
seasoning, onions, lemon juice, parsley
and mayonnaise. Refrigerate at least
½ hour. Top each muffin half with shrimp
mixture. Cover with a slice of Monterey
Jack cheese and broil 3-5 minutes, or
until cheese is melted and bubbly.
Serves 4. A great luncheon idea!

Shrimp Sandwich Spread

1 can tiny Pacific shrimp
  (or ½-1 cup fresh-cooked)
reserved juice from shrimp
1-8 oz. package cream cheese, softened
¼ cup chopped black olives
¼ cup chopped celery
⅛ cup chopped green onion
lemon juice to taste

Add juice from shrimp to cream
cheese. Blend with mixer until
smooth and creamy. Add remaining
ingredients and chill. If mixture
becomes too thick, add a little milk
(about 1 Tblsp.) and blend 'til smooth.
Spread on your favorite sandwich
bread and top with alfalfa sprouts,
or add shredded lettuce and stuff
into Pita (pocket) bread. Makes
about 2 cups.

Shrimp Bake

1 cup melted butter
dash garlic salt
1/3 cup fresh-snipped
  parsley
1/2 tsp. paprika
dash cayenne pepper

2/3 cup sherry
5½ cups cooked,
  peeled, cleaned
  shrimp
2 cups soft bread
  crumbs

Add garlic, parsley (reserve 2 Tblsp.), paprika, cayenne and sherry to melted butter. Stir well; add bread crumbs and toss. Spoon mixture over shrimp in 9x13 pan. Bake 20-25 minutes at 350°F. Sprinkle remaining parsley over the top. Serves 8-10.

Shrimp and Eggs

½ lb. cooked, peeled.
   cleaned shrimp
3 slices bacon
½ cup chopped green
   pepper
½ cup chopped onion
½ tsp. salt

⅛ tsp. cayenne
6 eggs, beaten
¼ cup cream
1 tsp. Worcestershire

Cut large shrimp in half. Fry bacon 'til crisp; drain and crumble. Cook green pepper and onion in bacon drippings until tender. Add shrimp and seasonings ; heat through. Combine eggs, cream, Worcestershire and bacon. Add to shrimp mixture and cook until firm, stirring occasionally. Serves 6.

Shrimp Quiche

¼ lb. bacon
½ cup onion, chopped fine
½ lb. Gruyere cheese, grated
5 eggs, slightly beaten
2 cups half and half
½ tsp. salt

dash cayenne
dash nutmeg
1 tsp. fresh-snipped parsley
1 cup tiny Pacific shrimp
pastry for single 9" pie crust

Cook bacon until crisp. Crumble and set aside. Reserve 1 Tblsp. bacon fat. Cook onion in reserved fat until golden. Line a 9" pie pan with pastry and bake 5 minutes at 450°F. Remove from the oven and sprinkle with bacon, onion and grated cheese. Mix together eggs, half and half, cayenne, nutmeg and parsley. Pour into pie shell. Add shrimp. Bake 10 minutes at 450°F., then reduce heat to 325°F. and bake until firm (about 30 minutes) or until knife inserted in the center comes out clean. Cut into pie-shaped wedges and serve. Serves 6.

Plain Pastry

1 cup flour   dash salt
1/4 cup <u>cold</u> water
1/3 cup plus 1 Tblsp.
  shortening

Combine flour and salt. Cut in
shortening with pastry cutter or fork.
Blend until mixture forms small balls
about the size of peas. Add water,
shape into ball and roll out on floured
board. Makes pastry for single 9" pie
crust. (Add 1/4 cup grated Swiss or
Cheddar cheese and 1 tsp. fresh-snipped
thyme to flour when preparing seafood
or vegetable pies, if you like. A nice
added flavor that also lends eye appeal!)

Sweet and Sour Shrimp

2 Tblsp. cornstarch
3 Tblsp. brown sugar
1 cup chicken broth
2/3 cup pineapple juice
1/4 cup vinegar
2 Tblsp. soy sauce
1/4 tsp. Chinese Five
    Spice

1 Tblsp. butter
1-7oz. pkg. frozen
    peapods
2 cups shrimp
2½ cups hot cooked
    rice

Thaw peapods. Blend cornstarch and brown sugar in saucepan; stir in chicken broth. Add pineapple juice, vinegar, soy sauce, Chinese Five Spice and butter. Cook and stir until mixture comes to a boil. Cover and simmer 3 minutes. Add peapods and shrimp and heat through. Serve over hot cooked rice or serve in molded rice ring. Serves 4-5.

Oysters

Classified as mollusks, oysters are a very popular shellfish. Not only are they high in food value and flavor, they are easily digestible and highly nourishing. Their composition is similar to milk in that they are rich in vitamins and minerals. When you buy oysters, look for firm, plump meats. They have a natural creamy color and a minimum of clear liquid. Poor handling and packaging results in an excessive amount of liquid, bloating, fewer oysters per package and some loss of flavor and food value. Graded and sold according to size, the smaller oysters are more expensive. Cuts (imperfect oysters) are a better buy for that favorite oyster stew.

For those of you who are beachcombers and enjoy picking your own oysters directly off of the beach, please consider this. The shells that encase those tasty morsels are homes for many more oysters. That's right! There are approximately fourteen days during the summer months when the oysters "spawn". The tiny spat fill the waters. Those that aren't eaten by other sealife, catch or attach themselves to rocks or other oyster shells. If you observe an oyster shell very carefully, you will see tiny specks and maybe even other small oyster shells. The specks are actually oyster seed or "spat", and the other small oyster shells have life in them, too.

Both will continue to grow but only if they are returned to the saltwater within a short time. Please check with local fish and game officials regarding laws requiring you to shuck oysters on the beach and return shells to the water.

<u>To shuck an oyster</u>: You'll need a heavy glove and a sharp oyster knife. Protect your oyster-holding hand with the glove. Hold the oyster bowl side down on a cutting board. Insert the rounded point of the knife near the curve. Push the blade into the cavity, keeping the point down against the inside of the lower shell and the handle up. Twist the knife back and forth to cut the abductor muscle. When this muscle is cut, the shell will open. Cut away the top abductor muscle to remove the meat.

← bowl side down

Oyster Stuffing

¼ cup minced onion
¼ cup diced celery
½ cup bacon drippings
4 cups whole-wheat
   bread cubes
½ tsp. salt
⅛ tsp. pepper

⅛ tsp. mace
⅛ tsp. thyme
1 pint extra small
   oysters
¼ cup oyster liquid
1 Tblsp. lemon juice

Sauté onion and celery in bacon drippings.
Add bread cubes and seasonings. Mix
lightly with a fork. Parboil oysters 3 minutes.
Drain, reserving ¼ cup oyster liquid. Add
oysters, reserved liquid and lemon juice
to bread mixture. Excellent for turkey,
chicken, game hens, pork rib chops or
baked casserole-style all by itself. It makes
an everyday meal a special occasion.
Makes about 6 cups.

Wild Oyster Pie

pastry for two-crust pie   salt and pepper
1 pint small oysters   lemon juice
1½ cups cooked wild rice   2 Tblsp. butter

Line a shallow pie plate with pastry.
Parboil oysters for 3 minutes; drain. Place
two layers of oysters in pie shell. If you
have more than two layers the middle
ones will be underdone. Fill in with hot
cooked wild rice. Sprinkle with salt,
pepper and lemon juice. Dot with butter,
cover with pastry and prick well. Bake at
400°F. until golden brown, about 20 minutes.
For added flavor, include ½ tsp. seafood
seasoning and 1 tsp. parsley flakes in your
pie crust. Serve hot or cold. Terrific with
sliced ham. Serves 4-6.

Br - Oysters

2 dozen small oysters
  on the half-shell
1" bacon cubes
⅓ cup butter

¼ tsp. salt
1½ Tblsp. parsley
3 drops hot sauce
2 Tblsp. lemon juice

Arrange oysters in shallow baking dish or broiler pan. Top each with a cube of bacon and broil 5-7 minutes under medium heat. Additional time will be needed if oysters are larger. Cream together remaining ingredients. Place a dab of butter mixture on each oyster. Return to broiler for 1 minute. Serve hot. Serves 4.

Cooked Oyster Cocktail

1 qt. cooked oysters
1 cup catsup
1 cup chili sauce
2 Tblsp. grated onion
½ tsp. tabasco sauce
2 Tblsp. Worcestershire

½ tsp. lemon juice
½ tsp. horseradish
salt and pepper
parsley sprigs
lemon wedges

Refrigerate oysters until cool. Combine remaining ingredients. Refrigerate to blend flavors. Just before serving, layer oysters, sauce, oysters, sauce, etc. in cocktail glasses. Top with parsley sprigs and lemon wedges. 8-10 servings.

Deep Fried Oysters

2 pts. small oysters   hot deep fat (370°F.)
thin batter mix (prepared)   lemon juice

Parboil oysters 3 minutes, drain and
cool. Dip in batter mix and deep fry
until golden brown. Remove with slotted
spoon and drain on paper towels. Sprinkle
with lemon juice. Serve with your
favorite condiments; cocktail sauce,
tartar sauce, creole sauce (see SAUCES).
Serves 4.

Thin Batter Mix

1 cup flour   ¾ cup milk
¼ tsp. salt   1 tsp. oil
2 eggs, beaten   1 tsp. lemon juice

Sift together flour and salt. To beaten
eggs add milk, oil and lemon juice. Add
flour and salt and stir until moistened.

Dad's Oyster Stew

½ gallon oysters ("cuts" will do nicely)
water enough to cover
4 tsp. soda
2 cups half and half
3 Tblsp. dehydrated onion

4 Tblsp. butter
salt and pepper
parsley sprigs

Bring oysters to a boil in soda water. Reduce heat and simmer. Skim froth from the top. Continue to cook and skim until liquid is clear and frothing subsides. Add half and half, onion, butter, salt and pepper. Heat through. Do not boil. Garnish with parsley sprigs. Serves 8-10.

Steamed Oysters on the Halfshell

2 dozen small to medium oysters in the shell
(You will have better success with single
oysters. Try to avoid clusters of 2 or more oysters.)

Clean oysters by rinsing any sand or mud
from the shells. Use a small vegetable brush
if necessary. Place oysters in baking dish -
"bowl" side down - in 1" of water. Cover with
foil. Bake at 500°F. for 35-40 minutes, or until
shells have popped open. Remove lids from
shells. Arrange on a serving tray and serve
with melted butter and a dash of tabasco
if desired. Entree for 2 or appetizers for 4.

This method of cooking oysters may also
be done on a barbecue over hot coals either
in a baking dish or directly on the grid.
You can also microwave your oysters in
the shell being certain to use a glass or
other microwave-safe dish and plastic
wrap in place of the foil. Reduce cooking
time to 10 minutes on high heat, longer
if necessary for shells to pop open.

Scalloped Oysters

2 pints small oysters
2 beaten eggs
cracker meal
½ tsp. seafood seasoning
1 small minced onion
¼ cup celery, chopped
   fine
½ tsp. thyme

½ cup evaporated
   milk mixed
   with ½ cup water
3 Tblsp. butter
½ cup buttered
   crumbs

Parboil oysters for 3 minutes in enough water to cover. Drain and cover. Butter large shallow casserole dish. Dip oysters in egg and roll in cracker meal. Combine seafood seasoning, onion, celery and thyme. Arrange oysters in layers in casserole dish and season each layer with seafood seasoning, onion, celery and thyme mixture. Add any left over egg to milk, pour over oysters and dot with butter. Sprinkle buttered crumbs over the top and bake at 425°F. for 30 minutes. Serves 4.

Panfried Oysters

1 quart small-medium
   oysters
½ cup flour
1 tsp. seafood seasoning
⅛ cup shortening

⅛ cup margarine
lemon wedges
parsley sprigs

Parboil oysters for 3 minutes in enough water to cover. Drain. Put flour and seafood seasoning in a paper or plastic bag. Shake oysters in seasoned flour until coated. Panfry in shortening and margarine over medium-high heat. Turn after 3-5 minutes. Fry until golden brown. Serve with lemon wedges and trim with fresh parsley sprigs. Serves 4-6. Try a condiment tray with cocktail sauce, tartar sauce and oyster sauce (see SAUCES), and let your guests choose their own.

Angels on Horseback

shelled fresh oysters
strips of thinly sliced bacon

Rinse oysters in cold water. Parboil
for 3 minutes. Drain and dry between
paper towels. Wrap a thin strip of bacon
around each oyster; fasten with tooth-
picks. Place oysters on broiler rack in
hot oven and roast until bacon is brown
and crisp. Serve on hot buttered toast.
For an added touch, use lemon butter
(see SAUCES) on toast and sprinkle with
parsley flakes. Super as hors d'oeuvres
or as a light lunch.

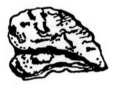

Pickled Oysters

1 cup vinegar	3 cups water
⅔ cup brown sugar	2 Tblsp. salt
⅓ cup mixed pickling spice	1 quart small
1 large white onion, sliced	oysters

Parboil oysters 3 minutes; drain. Combine vinegar, brown sugar, pickling spice, water and salt in saucepan; boil 5 minutes. Pour while hot over cooked oysters and raw onion rings. (1 layer oysters, 1 layer onion rings, etc.) Cover and let stand in cool place. Sliced hard-boiled eggs may be added if desired.

Thyme for Sautéed Oysters

1 pint extra small oysters	½ tsp. garlic
3 Tblsp. butter or margarine	powder
½ tsp. thyme	

Rinse oysters in ice cold water, drain and pat dry. Melt butter in saucepan over medium heat. Add thyme and garlic powder. Place oysters in pan in single layer; turn to coat with seasoned butter. Sauté over medium heat for 5-7 minutes, turning periodically. Serves 2. (If you grow your own herbs, try fresh snipped lemon thyme!)

Oyster Snaps

24 small fresh oysters
¼ cup wine vinegar
2 Tblsp. soy sauce
½ cup cashews, ground fine
½ cup mayonnaise
1 tsp. lemon juice

1 Tblsp. soy sauce
½ tsp. Chinese Five
   Spice
½ tsp. sugar
2 slices bacon, cut
   in 1" pieces

Drain liquid from oysters and blend with vinegar and 2 Tblsp. soy sauce. Pour over oysters and marinate 10 minutes. Drain and roll in cashews. Lightly butter bottom of shallow baking pan. Arrange oysters in a single layer just slightly apart. Blend mayonnaise, lemon juice, remaining 1 Tblsp. soy sauce, Chinese Five Spice and sugar. Place 1 teaspoon of the mixture on each oyster. Top with bacon pieces. Broil 3 inches from the heat for 5 minutes or until oysters start to curl at edges and bacon sizzles. Serve on buttered toasted muffins or your favorite crackers. Appetizers for 4-6.

Oysters Rockefeller

36 small-medium oysters
in the shell
2 cups cooked spinach,
chopped
6 Tblsp. minced onion
2 tsp. fresh snipped thyme
1½ Tblsp. fresh snipped parsley

½ tsp. celery salt
¼ tsp. salt
8 drops tabasco
½ cup bread
crumbs
8 Tblsp. butter

Preheat oven to 400°F. Open oysters and drain. Place each oyster on bowl half of shells. Combine spinach, onion, parsley and seasonings. Cook in butter for 3 minutes. Add bread crumbs and mix well. Spread mixture over oysters and bake for 8-10 minutes. Serves 4-6.

Smoked Oysters

Brine: 1 cup salt
2 cups brown sugar
1½ quarts water

1 gallon oysters –
use medium
to large as they
will shrink

Bring brine to a boil and add 1 gallon oysters. Bring just to boiling and drain. Smoke oysters over alder chips for 2-3 hours. An excellent dry smoke; no added oil.

Clams

Clams are best, of course, when you dig them yourself. Take off your shoes, roll up your pant legs and sleeves and DIG! To get the most flavor from your clams, keep them alive. After soaking in seawater overnight, place clams on a screen, rack or bed of seaweed to allow excess moisture to drip away. Cover clams with a burlap bag that has been soaked in seawater. Resoak the bag every few hours and your clams will stay fresh for several days. Also, be aware that fresh water will kill clams within an hour or two.

If you can't dig them, clams can be bought fresh, frozen or in the can (any time) in most retail seafood outlets.

Clams can be frozen quite successfully in the shell with a few hints in mind. If you dig them yourself, always soak clams overnight in a bucket of seawater. This will allow them to pump out any sand left inside. Secondly, freeze them fresh. If their shells are still shut tight or you see some activity, they are alive and still freezable. If their shells have sprung open, they have died and are best ground for chowder or fritters within a short time. However, as with any seafood, the fresher the better!

Here you will find recipes that show the versatility of clams and clam nectar.

clam

Native littleneck

Japanese littleneck

Butter clam

Cockle

<u>Native littleneck</u> - creamy gray or mottled brown shells with rings and ridges depicting a cross-hatch design

<u>Japanese littleneck</u> - similar in size and appearance to the Native littleneck, but slightly more oblong. Sometimes called the manila, the Japanese littleneck is distinguishable by a deep purple color on the inside of the shell near the siphon.

<u>Butter clam</u> - grows up to five inches in length. They are larger than the littlenecks with extremely heavy, thick shells marked with rings.

<u>Cockles</u> - beautiful, deeply corrugated fan-shaped shells. Collectors love them!

Clam Dip

2 - 8oz. pkgs. cream
   cheese, softened
3 cans (each 6½ oz.)
   chopped clams, drained
   (reserve ¼ cup liquid)
3 Tblsp. onion, chopped fine
2 Tblsp. beer

¼ cup ripe olives,
   chopped fine
2 tsp. Worcestershire
2 tsp. lemon juice
½ tsp. tabasco

Beat cream cheese in large bowl 'til smooth and creamy. Add remaining ingredients and blend well. Refrigerate for several hours to blend flavors, and serve as a dip with crackers or corn chips.

Or, pour into hollowed-out party loaf, top with bread lid, wrap in foil and bake 2-3 hours at 250°F. Serve with vegetables and bread chunks. Serves 12.

Clam Fritters

2 cups shucked clams
   (butters or littlenecks)
1⅓ cups all-purpose flour
2 tsp. baking powder
¾ tsp. salt
¼ tsp. pepper

shortening or
  oil
½ cup clam nectar
3 drops tabasco
2 eggs, slightly
  beaten

Coarsely chop clams. Sift together flour, baking powder, salt and pepper. Stir in chopped clams combined with clam nectar, tabasco and eggs. Drop by tablespoonsful into a hot skillet, slightly greased or oiled. Fry until golden brown on both sides. Makes about 2 dozen.

Buttery Broiled Clams on the Halfshell

3 dozen medium to large clams on the
 halfshell
5 slices bacon, cut into 1" pieces
⅓ cup butter, creamed
1½ Tblsp. fresh snipped parsley
¼ tsp. garlic salt
3 drops hot sauce
2 Tblsp. lemon juice

Arrange clams in shallow broiler pan
or baking dish. Top each with a piece
of bacon and broil 5-7 minutes under
medium heat. Make sure bacon is crisp.
Blend parsley, garlic salt, hot sauce and
lemon juice into creamed butter. Dot
each clam with a little butter mixture
and place under broiler for 1 minute.
Serve hot with hot, fresh rolls, coleslaw
and hot seasoned clam nectar. Serves 4-6.

Steamed Clams with Lemon Butter

7-10 lbs. littleneck clams in the shell
water enough to cover half the clams
Lemon Butter (see SAUCES)

Put water and clams in a large pot.
Cover and simmer until the clam shells
have opened. With slotted spoon, remove
clams to a serving bowl. Reserve clam
nectar (the broth left in the kettle
after steaming clams), strain and serve
in cups with a dash of salt and pepper.
Top with a pat of butter. To eat clams,
remove from shells with cocktail forks
and dip in Lemon Butter (served in
individual bowls). Place extra bowls on
the table for empty shells. A tasty meal
for those casual evenings anytime of
year. Serve with Cheesy Garlic Bread
(see Potpourri) and a tossed green salad.

Note: For best results, DO NOT THAW
CLAMS FROZEN IN THE SHELL BEFORE
COOKING. Plop frozen clams into water
and steam. Allow about 5 minutes
more cooking time.

New England Style Clam Chowder

½ lb. bacon, cut in 1" squares
½ cup onion, chopped
1 cup chopped celery
3-4 medium potatoes, diced
1½ cups diced carrots,
   about 3 medium
2 cups cold water
2 Tblsp. butter

5 cups clam
   nectar
2 cups chopped
   clams
salt and pepper
   to taste
1 Tblsp. parsley
3 cups light cream

Cook bacon until crisp. Remove and drain on paper towel. Reserve 2 Tblsp. bacon grease. Add onion and celery to reserved grease and sauté until tender. Combine water, clam nectar, bacon, onion, celery, potatoes, carrots, clams and seasonings in a large kettle. Bring to a boil; reduce heat and simmer until vegetables are tender, about 45 minutes. Just before serving, add light cream, parsley and butter. Heat through. Serves 6.

Note: For thicker chowder, to the 2 cups cold water add 4 Tblsp. flour and shake until well blended before adding to the other ingredients.

Manhattan Style Clam Chowder

2 cups clams and
   liquid
4 strips bacon, diced
1 medium onion,
   chopped
3 potatoes, peeled
   and diced
2 cups water
½ cup celery, chopped

1 can (16 oz.) stewed
   tomatoes
1 can (4 oz.) tomato
   paste
1 tsp. salt
⅛ tsp. pepper
⅛ tsp. thyme
⅛ tsp. basil
½ bay leaf

Sauté bacon in large kettle until crisp. Add onion and celery and cook until tender. Drain clams, reserving liquid. Add clam liquid, potatoes and water to bacon, onion and celery. Cook until potatoes are tender, about 10-15 minutes. Add clams, tomatoes, tomato paste and seasonings. Heat through. Serves 6-8.

Scallops

Scallops are another member of the mollusk group and are known to most everyone as a type of muscle. The marketed portion of a scallop is, in fact, the adductor muscle that controls the shell movement. It actually makes up less than ten percent of the whole scallop.

The large sea scallop is white, orange or pink in color and, because of its abundance, is used more in quantity food operations.

The smaller bay scallops, located in inland waters, are found in fewer numbers and are considered a delicacy. Bay scallops are creamy white, light tan or pinkish in color.

Both species have sweet, firm white meat and should have a sweetish odor before cooking. When bought in packages, they should be practically free of liquid.

Scallop Kabobs

Alternate large raw scallops, cleaned and deveined raw shrimp, bacon squares, mushroom caps and pineapple chunks on 6" skewers. Brush with melted butter flavored with onion powder and seafood seasoning. Broil 3-4 inches from heat, turning until golden; or grill over charcoal. Serve plain, with Cocktail Sauce (see SAUCES) or seasoned butter.

Proportions will depend on the number of people you are serving. Don't hesitate to figure at least 2 kabobs per person. They're delicious!

Scallops Dijon

1 lb. scallops
3 Tblsp. butter
1 tsp. Dijon mustard
1/4 tsp. salt

dash cayenne pepper
1/3 cup buttered soft
  bread crumbs

Parboil scallops for 2-3 minutes. Drain, reserving 1/3 cup liquid. Chop scallops. Cream together butter, mustard, salt and cayenne. Add reserved liquid and scallops. Let stand 1/2 hour to blend flavors. Put in baking dish, cover with bread crumbs and bake at 375°F. for 20 minutes. Serves 2.

Scallops in Wine and Cheese Sauce

1½ lbs. scallops
½ cup dry white wine
½ tsp. salt
dash cayenne pepper
1 tsp. minced onion
3 Tblsp. butter

1½ Tblsp. flour
½ cup heavy cream
1 cup grated sharp
  Cheddar cheese
½ cup buttered soft
  bread crumbs

Cut scallops in bite size pieces. Place in saucepan with wine, salt, cayenne and onion. Bring to a boil and simmer, covered, for 10 minutes. Drain, reserving broth. Melt butter and blend in flour. Add reserved broth and cream. Stir over low heat until thickened. Stir in cheese and scallops. Divide into individual baking dishes. Top with crumbs. Bake 10 minutes at 400°F. Elegant and rich! Serves 6.

Scallops Under Cover

1 qt. scallops   ½ lb. thinly sliced bacon

Parboil scallops (split larger ones) in their own liquid or water until they begin to shrink, approximately 3 minutes. On a rack in a shallow baking pan, place a layer of bacon and a layer of scallops and cover with a second layer of bacon. Bake at 350°F. until bacon is crisp and scallops have lost their translucency. Serve on a bed of hot, cooked brown rice tossed with sauteed onions and green peppers. Serves 4.

Scallops Romano

1½ lbs. scallops
5 Tblsp. butter
1 clove fresh garlic
⅓ cup dry white wine
¼ cup fresh parsley, chopped
1 tsp. salt

⅛ tsp. fresh ground pepper
1½ cups lightly toasted bread crumbs
2 Tblsp. melted butter
½ cup grated Romano cheese

Cut large scallops in half. Mince garlic and simmer in 5 Tblsp. butter for about 1 minute over medium heat. Add scallops and simmer about 3-5 minutes. Add wine and continue cooking another 3 minutes. Sprinkle with salt and pepper. Cover and simmer 5 minutes over low heat. Combine remaining 2 Tblsp. butter, parsley and bread crumbs. Sprinkle cheese over scallops ; top with bread crumb mixture. Cover and heat until cheese is melted and bubbly. Serve with rice or pasta. Serves 4.

Deep - Fried Scallops

1 qt. scallops
6 cups cold water
1 Tblsp. salt
2 eggs beaten into
   4 Tblsp. cold water

cracker crumbs
  seasoned with
  seafood seasoning
cooking oil
tartar sauce

Cut large scallops into ½" cubes. Immerse scallops for 3 minutes in salted water; drain. Dip scallops into egg-water mixture and roll in seasoned crumbs. Cook in deep fat at about 380°F. by placing a single layer of scallops in a frying basket, or use a slotted spoon to immerse and remove scallops from deep fat. Cook until golden brown in color. Serve with tartar sauce (see SAUCES). Serves 4.

Mussels

Anyone who has a boat ramp or dock, or has visited a marina or some favorite quiet coves, has probably seen the small Blue Mussels. They prefer quiet waters and, attached by threadlike structures, they cling to rocks, pilings and floats.

You can gather your own but, please, limit your harvesting to areas free of pollutants. For example, mussels harvested from creosoted pilings would not be a healthy catch.

The California Mussel, a larger species found on the open coastline, grows to 10 inches in length. However, be careful of this one. It is edible but, at certain times of year, it can cause paralytic shellfish poisoning. You may want to check with local officials before harvesting.

mussels

Baked Mussels

2-3 qts. mussels in the shell (scrubbed)
¼ cup water   ¼ cup dry white wine

Place mussels in large, shallow baking
pan. Pour in liquids. Cover with foil and
bake at 400°F. for 15 minutes or until
shells open. Discard any that don't open.
Serve with melted butter. Serves 4-6.

Mussels in Wine Sauce

4-5 dozen mussels in the shell   2 Tblsp. flour
1 Tblsp. minced onion   ¼ tsp. salt
1 clove garlic, crushed   ¼ tsp. pepper
¾ cup white wine   1½ tsp. fresh
6 Tblsp. butter   snipped parsley

Scrub mussel shells thoroughly. Place in
saucepan with onion, wine and garlic.
Simmer covered 6-10 minutes or until mussel
shells open. Remove top shell from each
mussel and arrange on a serving plate. Strain
liquid in saucepan. Cook until one third
original quantity. Cream together butter and
flour and add to liquid. Bring to a boil; add
salt and pepper. Pour over mussels and sprinkle
with parsley. A great beginning for a traditional
seafood buffet. Serves 6-8.

Steamed Mussels

1 clove garlic, minced
5 Tblsp. butter
⅓ cup onion, chopped fine
1 cup dry white wine
½ cup chicken broth

¼ cup snipped parsley
⅛ tsp. pepper
3 qts. fresh mussels in
  the shells, cleaned
a large kettle

Cook onion and garlic in butter until soft. Add wine, chicken broth and parsley and cook until mixture boils. Add mussels and simmer, covered, until mussels open, about 10 minutes. Throw away mussels that have not opened by this time. Transfer mussels to individual bowls and spoon broth over each serving. An excellent main dish for 2-3, or appetizers for 6-10.

Squid & Octopus

Squid and octopus are members of the mollusk family, but have no hard outer shell. Classified as cephalopods, they have sucker-bearing arms, highly developed eyes and a bag of inky fluid they can eject.

The squid has a long, soft body, ten arms surrounding the mouth, and a pair of fins that are triangular or round. Unlike the octopus, the squid has a transparent cuttlebone down the center of the back. The back is the side on which the eyes are most visible. The useful parts of the squid are the meaty body covering, or hood, the tentacles and the ink sac. The ink may be used in broths or stews. Squid can be purchased in most seafood markets and some grocery stores, fresh or frozen whole. Late winter through early spring is the prime season.

The octopus has a soft body with eight arms. The undersides of the arms have small parts that help them cling by suction. If it loses an arm, the octopus simply grows a new one. The octopus is a boneless creature and actually has three hearts. When excited, the octopus will change its color to match its feelings. It is not unusual for an octopus to turn blue, brown, gray, purple, red, white or even striped! The useful parts of the octopus are the body, the tentacles and the ink sac. You will find octopus at fish markets cleaned whole, fresh or frozen. You can also purchase it in some specialty stores canned or smoked. A real delicacy!

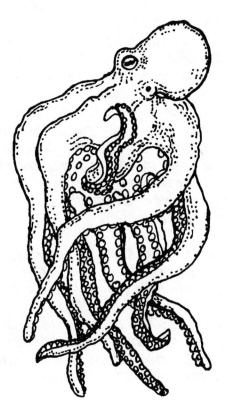

To Clean Whole Squid

1. Slip sharp point of knife just under thin, filmy membrane covering squid and make a slit. Film can then be easily removed by peeling or rubbing.

2. Lay squid, back side up, on the counter with tentacles fully extended. Push cuttlebone up and out toward head; discard.

3. Grasp head and tentacles with one hand, the hood (long, tube-like body) with the other. Pull, turning hood inside out to remove head and all internal organs. Be careful not to rupture the ink sac.

4. Cut off tentacles above eyes and ink sac. Spread tentacles open to expose center. Squeeze gently to pop out parrot-like beak from between tentacles; discard beak.

5. Rinse the hood and tentacles in cold water. Save the ink sac if you wish and discard the head and internal organs.

Squid Sauté

2 lbs. squid, cleaned
6 Tblsp. butter
2 cloves garlic, minced
¼ cup sweet red bell
   pepper, chopped fine

3 Tblsp. fresh
   basil leaves

Cut squid in rings by slicing cleaned whole hoods. Leave tentacles intact. Melt butter in large heavy skillet. Add garlic, bell pepper and basil. Sauté about 3 minutes. Add squid rings and tentacles. Cook and stir frequently for about 5 minutes over medium heat. Appetizers for 6 or add to hot cooked pasta as a main dish for 4.

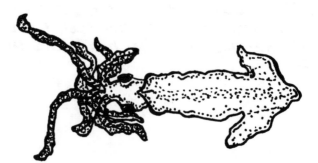

Stuffed Squid

2 lbs. squid, whole
   cleaned
1/4 cup white onion,
   minced
1- 15 oz. can spinach,
   drained or
1 pkg. frozen chopped
spinach, thawed and
drained
2 chicken bouillon
   cubes, crumbled
1/2 tsp. garlic powder
1/8 tsp. thyme

1 1/2 cups small curd
   cottage cheese
2 eggs, slightly
   beaten
1/2 cup sharp
   Cheddar, grated
1- 16 oz. can Italian-
style stewed
tomatoes
1/2 cup Parmesan
   cheese, grated
1/2 cup Mozarella
   cheese, shredded

Mix onion, spinach, bouillon, garlic
powder, thyme, cottage cheese, eggs and
Cheddar. Fill squid hoods with spinach
mixture. Arrange in a single layer in
a greased 13x9x2 inch pan. Pour stewed
tomatoes over squid; sprinkle with
Parmesan and Mozarella. Bake in
350°F. oven for 30-35 minutes. Serve with
curly vegetable pasta tossed with butter
and lightly seasoned with seafood
seasoning. Serves 4.

Squid Flower and Vegetable Stir-Fry

3 Tblsp. cooking oil
1 Tblsp. fresh ginger,
  minced
1 small, white onion,
  sliced thin
1 tsp. Chinese Five
  Spice
1 large carrot,
  sliced thin
2 stalks celery, cut
  diagonally

1-7oz. can bamboo
  shoots, drained
1½ lbs. whole squid,
  cleaned (*prepared)
¼ cup fresh-snipped
  marjoram leaves
3 Tblsp. white wine
  vinegar
1 tsp. brown sugar
2 Tblsp. soy sauce

Place a wok or large frying pan
over high heat. When pan is hot, add
oil, ginger, onion, Chinese Five Spice,
carrot and celery. Stir-fry 2-3 minutes.
Add bamboo shoots and stir-fry about
1 minute. Add the squid and stir-fry
just until it curls (about 2 minutes).
Add marjoram, vinegar, brown sugar
and soy sauce. Continue to stir-fry
about 1 minute. Serves 4.

* To Prepare Squid for Cooking:

Slice cleaned, whole hoods into 1-inch
lengths. Fringe one edge of each section
with ½ inch cuts about ¼ inch apart.
As the sections cook, they curl into
"flowers." Leave tentacles intact. Another
type of "flower"!

Fried Calamari (Squid)

3 lbs. squid, cleaned
½ cup flour
2 eggs, slightly beaten
  with 2 Tblsp. cold
  water
½ cup cooking oil

1¼ cups buttered
  bread crumbs
  lightly seasoned
  with lemon-herb
  seasoning

Toast crumbs by spreading evenly on cookie sheet and baking 5 minutes at 400°F. Cut down center of squid hoods and open flat. Slice into 1" strips. Leave tentacles whole. Pat dry. Dip in flour, egg and then in crumbs to coat evenly. Place on rack and let dry at room temperature for about 10 minutes. Heat oil in a large, heavy skillet over medium-high heat for 1 minute. Fry body pieces first, several pieces at a time, about 5 minutes until golden brown on both sides. Drain on paper towels and keep warm in oven. Fry tentacles about 2 minutes (careful, they spatter!). Serve with lemon wedges and tartar sauce (see SAUCES). Serves 6.

Sweet and Sour Octopus

2 small octopus
(about 4 lbs.), cleaned
1 small sweet red pepper,
 sliced
1 medium white onion,
 sliced
1 small green bell
 pepper, sliced
3 stalks celery, cut
 diagonally in 1 inch
 pieces
bean sprouts

SAUCE
¼ cup soy sauce
1 - 13¼ oz. can
 pineapple chunks
 with syrup
⅓ cup vinegar
¾ cup packed
 brown sugar
¼ tsp. ground
 ginger

Parboil octopus for about 15 minutes in water enough to cover. The outer skin will begin to split. Rinse and peel skin off under cold, running water. Cut in 1" pieces. Combine all ingredients for sauce and marinate octopus for 30 minutes. Heat 2 Tblsp. oil in heavy skillet or wok over high heat for 1 minute. Stir-fry vegetables for 2-3 minutes. Add octopus and sauce and cook 2-3 minutes. Combine 1 Tblsp. cornstarch and ⅓ cup cold water. Add to octopus-vegetable combo. Cook and stir until sauce thickens. Serve over hot, cooked rice. Serves 4-6.

Octo-bits

1 lb. octopus tentacles
1/3 cup pineapple juice
1/4 cup soy sauce
1 tsp. Chinese Five Spice
1/2 tsp. Liquid Smoke

Parboil octopus tentacles for 2-3 minutes. Drain. Peel outer skin under cold, running water. Slice lengthwise in thin strips. Combine remaining ingredients and marinate strips 1-3 hours. Place strips on racks in dehydrator and dry on high heat 1-2 hours, depending on the thickness. Or, place on rack in 200°F. oven for 1 hour. Terrific for snacks!

Stuffed Octopus

1 octopus (about one
   foot in overall length),
   cleaned
1 clove garlic, minced
1 cup mushrooms, chopped
2½ cups seasoned bread
   crumbs
1 Tblsp. fresh snipped
   parsley

½ tsp. salt
¼ tsp. pepper
¼ tsp. oregano
6 Tblsp. olive oil
lemon wedges
   for garnish

Cut off tentacles and chop fine.
Combine with remaining ingredients.
Stuff mantle with this mixture, sprinkle
lightly with more salt and pepper and
bake for 45 minutes at 315°. Garnish
with lemon wedges. Serves 6.

Octopus Rings

2-4 lbs. octopus, cleaned and skinned
miso (Japanese soybean paste)
soy sauce

    Parboil octopus to skin. Cut tentacles
into rings about ¼" thick. Slice body into
strips; roll into rings. Skewer with picks
and serve with miso and soy sauce as
condiments. Hors d'oeuvres for 10-12.

Fish

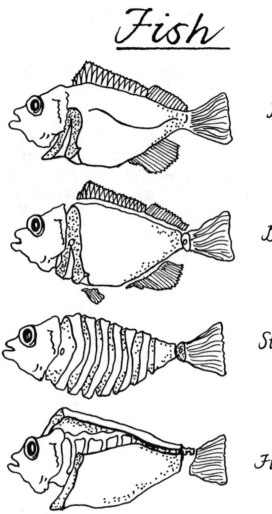

Drawn

Dressed

Steaks

Fillets

When preparing whole fish, leave head, tail, fins and scales intact if possible. These protective shields hold moisture and flavor in during cooking. If you are a bit squeamish about the head, remove before serving.

Cod

Of the 75 species of cod, only 2 live in fresh water. The others can be found on or near the bottom, in cold waters in all seas. There are three on the Pacific Coast : the Pacific Cod, the Pacific Tom Cod and the Pacific Pollock.

The Pacific Pollock is occasionally caught on hook and line. Because the flesh is fairly soft, however, fishermen generally don't seek it. In fact, it is often used as mink food.

The Pacific Cod is, on the other hand, probably the most abundant and considered the most important trawl-caught bottom fish in the Northern Pacific. Also known as the Gray Cod, it is marketed fresh and frozen, often as fish sticks.

The Pacific Tom Cod, although not so abundant as the Pacific Cod, is highly regarded for its wonderful flavor. The numbers and size of the Pacific Tom Cod don't allow for commercial fishing. Some are caught trawl-fishing for other species. You can catch them with baited hook and line or by jigging. When you do get a catch, prepare yourself for a real tasty treat!

Cod Creole

2 lbs. cod fillets
2 Tblsp. butter
¼ cup chopped onion
3 Tblsp. minced green
   pepper
1½ cups Italian style
   stewed tomatoes
¼ cup sliced fresh
   mushrooms

¼ tsp. salt
dash pepper
¼ tsp. basil
2 Tblsp. sherry
¼ cup sliced black
   olives

Cook onion and green pepper in butter until tender. Add tomatoes and mushrooms; cook 2 minutes. Add seasonings and sherry; remove from heat. Arrange fillets in baking dish. Pour sauce over fish and sprinkle with olives. Bake at 400°F. for 20 minutes. Serves 4-6.

Codfish Balls

2 cups cod, cooked
  and flaked
1 egg, beaten
dash pepper
1 Tblsp. melted
  butter

hot deep fat
1½ cups mashed
  potatoes
½ tsp. salt
½ Tblsp. onion juice

Mix cod, egg, pepper, butter, potatoes, salt and onion juice. Beat until smooth. Shape lightly into small balls and fry in hot (375°F.) deep fat until golden brown. Main dish servings for 4 or appetizers for 8-10.

Salt Cod Cakes

Boil ½ lb. of salt codfish until tender. Drain. Remove bones and shred finely. Mix with 2 cups mashed potatoes, 1 beaten egg, 1 Tblsp. milk and salt and pepper to taste. Make into cakes or balls. Dip in beaten egg then into crumbs. Fry over medium-high heat in butter until golden brown. Serves 2.

Linda Tucker's Cod Fillets Au Gratin

2 lbs. cod fillets
4 Tblsp. butter
1 cup bread crumbs
1 egg, slightly beaten
salt and pepper

¼ cup milk
lemon juice
chopped parsley
1 cup grated Monterey
Jack cheese

Melt butter and combine with bread crumbs. Spread on cookie sheet and toast in 400°F. oven for 5-10 minutes. Combine slightly beaten egg and milk. Dip fillets in egg-milk mixture. Roll in bread crumbs and lay out on baking sheet. Season lightly with salt and pepper. Sprinkle with lemon juice, chopped parsley and grated Monterey Jack cheese. Bake uncovered in 400°F. oven 10-15 minutes or until fish flakes easily when tested with a fork. Serves 4.

Codfish Salad

1½ cups cooked, boned
   and flaked codfish
¼ cup mayonnaise
¼ cup thousand island
   dressing
1 medium tomato, chopped
¼ cup diced celery
2 green onions, chopped
   fine
1 avocado, peeled and
   diced

¼ cup cucumber,
   peeled and
   diced
salad seasonings
   to taste
salt and pepper
2 hard-cooked
   eggs, sliced
lettuce leaves
paprika

Combine all ingredients except eggs,
lettuce and paprika. Chill at least
½ hour before serving on lettuce leaves.
Garnish with egg slices and sprinkle
with paprika. Serves 4.

Halibut

Halibut may be purchased all year 'round, fresh or frozen. The most economical way to buy halibut is in roasts or chunks. Here you will find recipes for preparing 3-5 lb. roasts, plus a variety of recipes using smaller amounts. Halibut may be baked, poached or cut into serving size pieces for broiling or frying. Allow ⅓ lb. of halibut for an average serving, which will supply up to ½ of the daily requirement of protein. Halibut provides a rich supply of nutrients with only about 175 calories per serving. Please remember, if you are using frozen halibut, do not thaw completely. Leave partially frozen. This will help retain moisture often lost in the cooking process.

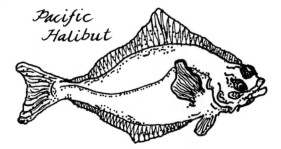

Pacific Halibut

Stuffed Halibut

1 3-4 lb. halibut roast
1 Tblsp. salt, divided
½ cup onion, chopped fine
¾ cup butter
⅓ cup chopped parsley
¾ cup diced celery
¼ tsp. thyme
¼ tsp. pepper
¼ tsp. seafood seasoning

⅓ cup coarsley chopped walnuts
2 hard-boiled eggs, chopped
2 cups cooked brown rice
2 Tblsp. milk

After rinsing and patting dry, rub halibut inside and out with half of the salt. Sauté onion in 3 Tblsp. butter. Add parsley, celery, thyme, pepper, seafood seasoning, nuts, eggs and rice. Moisten with milk. Fill halibut with stuffing mixture. Melt 1 Tblsp. butter in the bottom of baking pan. Place fish in pan and surround with any remaining stuffing mixture. Melt remaining butter and drizzle over the roast. Bake at 350°F. for 45-55 minutes or until fish is tender and flakes easily with a fork. Serves 6-8.

Halibut Cheeks Extraordinaire

2 lbs. halibut cheeks,
   fresh or frozen
¼ cup butter
1 clove minced garlic

¼ tsp. lemon pepper
½ cup dry white
   wine
1 tsp. parsley flakes

Rinse halibut cheeks in cold water; drain and cut into 1" cubes. Melt butter in medium saucepan. Add minced garlic, lemon pepper and parsley. Add halibut pieces, sauté 3-4 minutes, turning once. Add dry white wine and simmer another 2-3 minutes or until cheeks are tender and no longer transparent. Remove to heated serving tray. Serves 4.

Deep Fried Halibut Cheeks

2 lbs. halibut cheeks,
   cut in 1" cubes
2 Tblsp. lemon juice
salt
pepper

light batter *
hot deep fat (370°F.)
lemon wedges
tartar sauce (see
   SAUCES)

Rinse halibut cheeks in ice cold water. Pat dry. Sprinkle with lemon juice, salt and pepper. Dip in batter and deep-fry until golden brown. Drain on paper towel. Garnish with lemon wedges and serve with tartar sauce. Serves 4.

* Light Batter

Mix together :

1 egg, slightly beaten
½ cup water
½ cup flour

Whisk together until smooth.

Poached Halibut with Shrimp Sauce

2 lbs. halibut steaks
  or fillets
1 cup dry white wine
½ cup water
1 bay leaf
¼ tsp. thyme
½ tsp. salt
1½ cups reserved
  fish stock

2 Tblsp. cornstarch
  shaken in ¼ cup
  cold water
2 egg yolks, beaten
1 Tblsp. lemon juice
1 Tblsp. minced
  parsley
1 cup tiny Pacific
  shrimp

Place halibut in saucepan. Add wine, water and seasonings. Bring to a boil; reduce heat and simmer about 10 minutes or until halibut flakes easily with a fork. Carefully remove halibut and set aside. In seperate pan, pour in fish stock and cornstarch mixture. Heat and cook until smooth and creamy; stir constantly. Combine egg yolks, lemon juice and parsley. Whisk into fish stock. Add shrimp and simmer 5 minutes. Spoon sauce over halibut, reserve some to serve on the side. Serves 4-6.

Halibut Spread

1½ cups halibut,
   cooked and flaked
1 cup sour half and half
1 envelope dry onion
   soup
1 tsp. Worcestershire sauce

Combine all ingredients. Chill
thoroughly to blend flavors. Serve with
assorted crackers or raw vegetable
sticks. Makes 1⅔ cups spread.

Grilled Halibut Steaks

6 halibut steaks   1 tsp. salt
¼ cup melted butter   ⅛ tsp. pepper

    Combine butter and seasonings. Place steaks on greased grill or in well-greased wire broiler basket. Baste with butter. Grill over medium-hot coals for 5-8 minutes. Turn, brush with remaining butter and grill 5-8 minutes longer or until fish flakes easily with a fork. Sprinkle with parsley flakes and lemon juice. Serves 6.

Red Snapper

Red Snapper is a member of the rockfish family, commonly called rock cod. There are several species on the Pacific Coast.

Those found closer inshore are largely brown in color, while those in deep water, such as the snapper, tend to be red. So this one did acquire its name from its color, Red Snapper.

Their young are born alive during the summer months, in very large numbers, I might add! They are almost transparent at birth and their average length is about ½ inch.

These fish are fairly easy to catch if you find a "hole" and are generally close to the bottom. On the market, you will find Red Snapper either drawn whole or filleted.

red snapper

Citrus Snapper

1½ lbs. red snapper fillets
1 tsp. seafood seasoning
¼ tsp. pepper
¼ tsp. nutmeg

1 Tblsp. grated
  grapefruit rind
1 Tblsp. grated
  orange rind

Place rinsed snapper fillets in a
buttered baking dish. Sprinkle with
seasonings and grated fruit rinds.
Cover with foil and bake 15 minutes at
400°F. Serves 4.

Red Snapper Roll-ups

4 8-oz. snapper fillets
8 stalks fresh asparagus,
   (tough ends removed),
   steamed
1 can undiluted cream
   of shrimp soup

lemon pepper
paprika
Parmesan
   cheese
¼ cup half-and-
   half

Pre-heat oven to 350°F. Season fresh fillets lightly with lemon pepper. Roll each around 2 stalks steamed asparagus. Blend shrimp soup with half-and-half until smooth and creamy. Place roll-ups in shallow baking dish; cover with shrimp soup mixture. Sprinkle with Parmesan and paprika. Bake uncovered 20-30 minutes. Serves 4.

Poached Red Snapper

6 6-8 oz. snapper fillets
salt
fresh ground pepper
1 cup light-bodied
 red wine
4 Tblsp. butter
¼ cup chopped onion
⅛ cup chopped green
 pepper
2 cloves garlic, minced
¼ cup tomato sauce
2 Tblsp. minced parsley

¼ tsp. oregano
¼ tsp. thyme
¼ tsp. rosemary
1 tsp. cornstarch
 dissolved in
2 Tblsp. cold water
black olives (garnish)
cherry tomatoes
 (garnish)
fresh parsley
 sprigs

Pre-heat oven to 400°F. Rinse fillets in cold water, pat dry and place in single layers in two 9x13 baking dishes. Sprinkle with salt and pepper. Pour wine over fillets, cover and bake 10-15 minutes. Transfer carefully to platter. Measure liquid to equal 1 cup, adding wine if necessary. Set aside. Melt butter in saucepan over medium heat. Sauté onion until transparent; add garlic. Stir in reserved liquid, tomato sauce, parsley, oregano, thyme and rosemary. Bring to a boil, reduce heat and add cornstarch. Simmer, stirring constantly until thickened. Add fillets. Cover and refrigerate to bake later or bake covered 15-18 minutes at 350°F. Garnish. Serves 4-6.

Salmon

Salmon are the heart of the West Coast's fishing industry. There are five species of Pacific salmon that make up this most valuable market. These include the Sockeye, also known as the Red salmon in Alaska or the Blueback on the Columbia River. The Chinook is also referred to as the King, Spring, Tyee or Blackmouth. There is also the Pink or Humpback, the Coho or Silver and the Chum salmon. Of these, the Chinook is the largest and the Pink the most abundant. The Chum salmon is a particularly good fish for smoking and/or canning. Its light pink flesh becomes almost white in the process. Its nutritive value is equal to other salmon except for its lower oil content.

All species are anadromous. They are hatched in fresh water, and move to salt water until they attain their full growth. When fully mature, the salmon return to fresh water to spawn. Because of their natural homing instinct, almost all return to their streams of origin.

salmon

Salmon Sandwich Spread

2 cups cooked, flaked
   salmon
1/4 cup minced onion
1/3 cup grated carrot
1/3 cup mayonnaise
1/4 cup pickle relish

2 Tblsp. catsup
1 tsp. lemon juice
1/8 tsp. pepper
1/2 tsp. seafood
   seasoning

Combine all ingredients and chill.
Excellent spread on freshly baked dill
rye or any of your favorite sandwich
breads. Makes about 3 cups.

Salmon Loaf

2 cups cooked, flaked
   salmon
1 1/2 cups soft bread
   crumbs
3 Tblsp. melted butter
1/4 tsp. seafood seasoning

2 eggs, beaten
1/2 cup milk
1/4 tsp. thyme
salt and pepper
   to taste

Combine all ingredients. Form into loaf
and bake in well-oiled pan about 35 minutes
at 350°F. Serve with Egg Sauce, Convenient
Mushroom Sauce or Creole Sauce (see SAUCES).
Serves 4.

Salmon Pie

2 cups cooked, flaked
   salmon
½ tsp. seafood seasoning
½ cup buttered bread
   crumbs
3 hard-cooked eggs,
   sliced
⅓ cup onion, chopped
   fine

¼ cup milk
2 Tblsp. butter
1 tsp. parsley
   flakes
stuffed olives,
   sliced

Mix salmon and seafood seasoning.
Fill a well-oiled pie plate with
alternate layers of salmon, egg, onion
and crumbs. Dot with butter. Add milk.
Sprinkle with parsley flakes. Bake at
350°F. for about ½ hour. Garnish with
sliced stuffed olives. Serves 4-6.

Chilled Poached Salmon

1 4-8 lb. salmon (cleaned, head and tail intact)
2 large onions, sliced
15 whole black peppers
6 whole allspice
½ cup lemon juice or white wine vinegar

2 bay leaves
1 Tblsp. salt
2 cups dry white wine
4 qts. water

Combine all ingredients (except salmon) in poaching pan. Cover and simmer gently for 45 minutes. Wrap salmon snugly in cheesecloth, folding edges together on top. Place fish on the pan rack and lower into boiling liquid. Add water or wine to cover salmon, if necessary. Cover pan tightly with lid or foil. Simmer on top of stove, using 2 burners. Allow 10 minutes of cooking time for each 1" of thickness of fish. Place on platter; cool. Cover and chill at least 3 hours. Garnish with fresh parsley sprigs, lemon wedges and cherry tomatoes. Serves 8-12.

Baked Salmon Mousse

6 eggs
3 cups salmon, skinned
   and boned
1 cup heavy cream
1/4 cup dry white wine
1/4 cup drained capers
1 Tblsp. paprika

3/4 tsp. salt
1/4 tsp. black pepper
1/2 cup scallions,
   sliced thin
1/4 cup chopped
   parsley

In a large bowl combine salmon, cream, wine, capers, paprika, salt and pepper. Blend one-third of the mixture at a time, breaking 2 eggs into the blender each time. Blend 10-15 seconds, until mixture is smooth but salmon still has texture. Empty blender into a separate large bowl. Stir in scallions and parsley. Pour salmon into well-greased glass loaf pan or souffle dish. Set in baking pan. Pour boiling water into pan to a depth of 2 inches (to surround loaf pan or souffle dish, too). Bake in 350°F. oven for 1 hour, or until mousse is firm to touch. Serve hot in slices or wedges with Lobster Sauce (see SAUCES). To serve cold, chill and unmold before cutting into slices. Delicious with Horseradish Cream (see SAUCES). Serves 6.

NOTE: Tuna may be substituted for salmon if desired.

Deborah's Smoked Salmon Dip

1 lb. smoked salmon,
   skinned and boned
¼ tsp. Liquid Smoke
   (more or less to taste)
1 tsp. prepared horseradish

8 oz. cream
   cheese, softened
½ tsp. garlic salt
chopped nuts
parsley flakes

Combine smoked salmon, Liquid Smoke, horseradish, cream cheese and garlic salt in mixer bowl. Roll into large ball or individual logs. Roll in chopped nuts and parsley flakes. Serve on those special occasions with crackers or chips. Delightful!

Salmon Baked in Mayonnaise

2 lbs. salmon fillets
½ tsp. salt
1 cup real mayonnaise
½ tsp. celery salt
½ tsp. dill weed

1 Tblsp. grated onion
dash cayenne pepper
1 Tblsp. white vinegar
1 lemon, sliced thin
fresh parsley sprigs

Sprinkle fillets with ½ tsp. salt. Place on foil (skin side down) in a shallow baking dish. Combine mayonnaise and seasonings; spread over salmon. Bake at 350°F. for 20-30 minutes or until salmon flakes easily with a fork. Garnish with lemon slices and parsley sprigs. Serves 4.

Sole

Sole is a versatile, mild-flavored white fish and a member of the right-eyed flounders. A flat fish, its eyes and dark color are characteristically on the right side. Most live in cold waters. Of some 100 species, those most commonly marketed are the Petrale sole, Rex sole, Rock sole, Butter sole, Dover sole and English sole.

Mock Crab Salad

¼ lb. fresh crabmeat
1¾ cups cooked, flaked sole
lemon juice

salad greens
garnishes

Blend crabmeat and sole together in a small bowl. Cover and refrigerate overnight. Combine with lemon juice, salad greens and garnishes. For a delightful luncheon, serve with Thousand Island dressing and warm butterflake rolls. Main course for 4-6.

Almond-Crusted Sole

2 large fillets of sole,
   8 oz. each
⅓ cup sour cream
½ cup ground, blanched
   almonds
2 Tblsp. butter

1 Tblsp. oil
salt and pepper
   to taste
lemon wedges
parsley sprigs

Rinse fillets in cold water. Pat dry.
Season lightly with salt and pepper.
Spread with sour cream and coat with
almonds. Refrigerate for 1 hour. Sauté
in oil and butter over medium heat
approximately 5 minutes on each side.
Remove to serving platter; garnish with
lemon wedges and parsley sprigs. An
elegant dish for a romantic evening. Serve
with a semi-dry white wine. Serves 2.

sole

Raw Fish Seviche

1 lb. raw sole fillets
1 large, ripe tomato,
  peeled and sliced
1 large onion, sliced
  thin
5 hot chile peppers,
  whole
1 tsp. coriander seeds
1 cup tomato juice

2 cups lime juice
6 Tblsp. olive oil
¼ tsp. oregano
¼ cup dry white wine
salt to taste
red onion slices and
  parsley sprigs for
  garnish

Cut fillets into 1" squares. Combine remaining ingredients in medium-sized bowl. Add fish, spooning marinade over each piece. Cover and refrigerate overnight. Drain most of the liquid just before serving; garnish with a few red onion rings and fresh parsley sprigs. Serves 4-6. An appropriate appetizer for many occasions and always a great topic for conversation.

Broiled Fillet of Sole with Lemon Sauce

½ lb. sole per person,
   approximately
seafood seasoning
butter

lemon juice
parsley flakes
fresh parsley sprigs
Lemon Sauce

Rinse fillets in cold water. Place on foil-covered broiler rack. Sprinkle with lemon juice, seafood seasoning and parsley flakes and dot with pats of butter. Broil 5-7 minutes or until fish turns white and flakes easily with a fork. Do not overcook and do not turn fillets unless they are quite thick. Garnish with fresh parsley sprigs and serve with Lemon Sauce (see SAUCES).

Curried Sole Fillets

6 large sole fillets,
8 oz. each
1 cup grated coconut
1 cup milk
3 Tblsp. butter
¼ cup chopped onion

1 clove minced garlic
1½ Tblsp. curry powder
salt and pepper
Macadamia nuts
minced green onion

Preheat oven to 400°F. Combine coconut and milk in small saucepan. Simmer over medium heat until mixture foams, approximately 2 minutes. Put through strainer. Put a single layer of sole fillets in each of two 9x13 baking dishes. Pour coconut milk over fillets, cover and bake 10-15 minutes. Transfer fillets to a platter and allow to cool. Cover and chill. Drain liquid into small saucepan and cook to reduce to ¾ cup, stirring occasionally, about 10-12 minutes. Melt butter; add onion and garlic and sauté. Reduce heat, add curry powder and cook 5 minutes. Add the ¾ cup liquid and blend well. Simmer uncovered 8-10 minutes. Cool. Pour over fillets. Refrigerate to bake at a later time, or bake immediately, uncovered, at 350°F. for 10-12 minutes. Garnish with Macadamia nuts and minced green onion. Serves 4-6.

Tuna

Tuna are found worldwide in temperate and tropical seas. It's no wonder they've become such a popular food item. The tuna family includes true mackerels, Spanish mackerels, Bonitos and true Tunas. Many species migrate long distances and some are the backbone of major commercial fisheries. There are about 47 species in all. Probably the most familiar to you as a consumer are the Pacific Bonito, Albacore and Bluefin tuna.

The Pacific Bonito feed on small fish and squid. An excellent sport fish as well as an important commercial catch, the Pacific Bonito spawn in California waters from January to May. They come primarily from the Baja region, where they are canned.

Our only large tuna is the Bluefin. Most weigh 10-45 pounds. These range from Alaska to the Baja, but are most common south of Los Angeles. These fish are caught commercially as well as by sports fishermen.

It takes the Albacore about one year to migrate across the Pacific and it probably spawns midway. If you are interested in catching your own, the Pacific Coast fishing season is June through September. You'll see Albacore on many brands of canned tuna.

Tuna Pot Pie

2 cans (7½ oz. each)
  tuna, drained
¾ cup steamed,
  diced carrots
¾ cup cooked peas
¼ cup diced onion
salt and pepper

1 can cream of chicken-
  mushroom soup
½ cup water
crust for 2-crust pie

Line a 1 qt. casserole with pie crust. Bake
10 minutes. Break tuna into large pieces.
Combine tuna, carrots, peas and onion.
Sprinkle with salt and pepper to taste.
Combine soup and water in saucepan. Stir
over medium heat until smooth and
heated through. Pour over tuna mixture.
If sauce seems too thin, add 1 Tblsp. water
blended with 1 Tblsp. flour. Pour into
casserole and top with remaining pie crust.
Pierce and bake in pre-heated 450°F. oven
for 40 minutes or until golden brown.
Serves 4-6.

Deviled Tuna

3 English muffins,
    halved
3 cans (7½ oz. each)
    tuna, drained
¼ cup oil
¼ cup flour
½ tsp. salt

¼ tsp. tabasco
½ tsp. dry mustard
1 tsp. Worcestershire
2 cups milk
1 cup grated Cheddar

Place English muffins, cut side up, in shallow baking dish. Place under broiler until lightly toasted. Remove from broiler. Place one-half can flaked tuna on each muffin. Place in oven and bake at 450°F. for 7 minutes. Meanwhile, prepare sauce. Blend oil with flour, salt, tabasco, dry mustard and Worcestershire in saucepan. Add milk and cook, stirring constantly, until mixture thickens and comes to a boil. Add grated Cheddar; cook over low heat, stirring constantly, until melted. Remove tuna muffins from oven and spoon sauce over each serving. Place under broiler for 5 minutes or until lightly browned. Serves 6.

Tuna Burgers

2 cans (7½ oz. each)
  tuna, drained
1 can water chestnuts,
  chopped
¼ cup chopped black
  olives
⅓ cup minced onion
¼ cup bean sprouts
¼ cup fresh minced
  parsley

2 eggs, well beaten
½ tsp. garlic salt
½ tsp. seafood
  seasoning
½ tsp. oregano
¼ cup. oil
1 cup. grated Cheddar

Combine first 10 ingredients in medium bowl, mixing well. Refrigerate for ½ hour. Heat oil in large frying pan. Shape tuna mixture into patties. Fry in hot oil until golden brown, turning once. Top with grated Cheddar and cover for 2 minutes. Serve on English muffin rounds or Keyser rolls with lettuce and tomato slices. Serves 6.

Tomatoes Stuffed with Tuna Salad

1 - 7½ oz. can of tuna *
2 hard-cooked eggs,
   chopped
3/4 cup celery, chopped
¼ cup cucumber,
   chopped
1 Tblsp. grated onion

2 Tblsp. parsley flakes
1 Tblsp. lemon juice
⅓ cup mayonnaise
6 medium tomatoes
¼ tsp. salt
lettuce leaves

Drain and flake tuna. Combine all ingredients except tomatoes, salt and lettuce leaves. Cut tomatoes from the top halfway down, in wedges. Salt lightly and fill with tuna mixture. Serve in lettuce cups. Serves 6. A delightful luncheon with toasted muffin rounds.

* Other seafoods may be substituted for tuna, including salmon, crab or shrimp.

Potpourri

The following section includes a sampling of a variety of seafoods. One of these, the geoduck, is the largest clam on the Pacific Coast. You may need more than a little experience to dig these. They live at the lowest tide levels in muddy sand of protected bays, sometimes as deep as three feet below the surface. They are readily available at most seafood markets, sometimes whole, sometimes pre-packaged as steaks or ground for chowder or fritters.

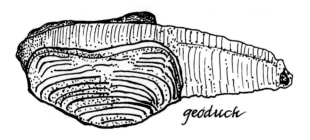

geoduck

Geoduck Chowder

½ lb. bacon, cut in 1" squares
½ cup onion, chopped
1 cup celery, chopped
3-4 medium potatoes, diced
2 cups water
5 cups clam nectar

3 medium carrots, grated
2 cups ground geoduck
salt and pepper to taste
3 cups milk
1 Tblsp. parsley flakes
2 Tblsp. butter

Cook bacon until crisp. Remove and drain on paper towel. Add onion and celery to bacon grease and sauté until tender. Combine water, nectar, bacon, onion, celery, potatoes, carrots, geoduck and seasonings in a large kettle. Simmer over low heat until potatoes are tender, about 30-40 minutes. Just before serving, add milk, parsley and butter. Heat through. Serves 6.

Geoduck Fritters

4 cups ground geoduck
2 cups flour
2 ½ tsp. baking powder
1 tsp. salt
cooking oil

¼ tsp. pepper
1 cup clam nectar
3 eggs, slightly
    beaten

Combine flour, baking powder, salt and pepper. Add ground geoduck combined with clam nectar and eggs. Mix well. Heat a little cooking oil in skillet. Drop geoduck mixture by tablespoonsful into hot oil and fry until golden brown on both sides. Remove to paper towels to drain, and serve hot with Tartar Sauce or your favorite seafood condiment (see SAUCES). Makes about 3½ dozen.

Pan-Fried Abalone

Pound slices of abalone with wooden mallet. Rinse with cold water and dry with paper towel. Dip in slightly beaten egg, then fine cracker crumbs. Sprinkle lightly with salt and pepper. Brown quickly in hot olive oil or butter, allowing about 30 seconds on each side. Do not overcook as abalone will toughen very quickly.

Crisp-Coated Abalone

1 lb. abalone, sliced thin and pounded	3 Tblsp. oil
1 cup cornflake crumbs	2 Tblsp. butter
	seafood seasoning

Rinse abalone in ice cold water. Pat dry. Roll in cornflake crumbs. Heat oil and butter in skillet over medium-high heat until hot. Brown abalone no more than 30 seconds on each side. Sprinkle with seafood seasoning to taste. Serve immediately. Serves 2.

Bouillabaisse

5 slices bacon
1 large onion, chopped
1/3 cup chopped parsley
1 clove garlic
2 cups clam nectar
1 cup water
1 cube chicken bouillon
dash lemon pepper
1 tsp. seafood seasoning
salt to taste
2 large potatoes, peeled
   and diced
1-12 oz. can whole
   tomatoes

1 lb. scallops
1 lb. halibut, cut in
   1" cubes
1 pt. extra small oysters,
   parboiled 3 minutes
2 cups milk
1 cup cream
12 littleneck clams,
   in shells
1 lb. prawns
1/2 lb. crabmeat
1/2 cup lobster meat,
   cut in pieces

In extra large kettle, cook bacon until crisp. Remove and set aside. Add onion, parsley and garlic to bacon drippings. Cook until onion is transparent. Add clam nectar, water, bouillon cube, seasonings, potatoes and tomatoes. Cover and simmer 20-30 minutes. Then add scallops, halibut and oysters. Simmer again for about 10 minutes. Add milk, cream, clams, prawns, bacon (crumbled), crabmeat and lobster. Cook until heated through, stirring often. Keep below boiling point. To thicken, add 1/4 cup flour blended with 1/4 cup cold water and continue cooking. A complete meal in itself. Serves 4-6.

Fish-Head Chowder

Absolutely delectable, with or without the eyes! This hearty soup boasts the best part of the fish - the heads. Sound crazy? Well, believe it when you try it. The best-tasting meat is found in the fish heads. The stock is made from the heads, backbones and other parts of the fish (after cleaning) that are usually thrown away. An economical and very nutritious meal. This can be made in large quantities and frozen in meal-size containers. You may prefer to call this fish chowder for the sake of any squeamish dinner guests. Have fun with this one and don't be afraid to experiment. You can't go wrong!

Fish Head Chowder

fish heads (preferably
  salmon) backbones, etc.
  (fresh)
6-8 slices bacon
1 large onion, cut in
  large pieces
3 cloves garlic, crushed
2 large cans whole
  tomatoes
4 large carrots, sliced
4 medium potatoes,
  diced
2 Tblsp. parsley

4 stalks celery,
  cut in large
  pieces diagonally
½ tsp. rosemary
1 tsp. seafood
  seasoning
½ tsp. thyme
salt and pepper
  to taste
water enough to
  cover several
  heads

Cover fish heads with water in large kettle. Add a few celery leaves and onion rings. Cover and simmer until heads are soft and begin to fall apart. Sauté bacon, onion and garlic in separate pan. Remove fish heads and bones from kettle. Add bacon pieces, onion and garlic to stock. Add tomatoes, vegetables and seasonings. Cover and simmer until vegetables are tender, about 30 minutes. Add meat from heads, etc. Cover and simmer another 5 minutes. Makes about 3 quarts.

Fried Saltwater Smelts

Clean smelts, leaving heads and tails intact. Generally, they are quite small (and exceptionally delicious), so allow a generous amount per person. Sprinkle smelts with salt and pepper. Roll in cornmeal or flour, dip in slightly beaten egg, then roll in cornmeal or flour again. Heat 2 Tblsp. margarine and 2 Tblsp. shortening in cast-iron skillet 'til hot. Fry smelts 3-5 minutes, turning once. Reduce heat slightly if smelts seem to be browning too quickly. Serve with hard rolls and tartar sauce (see SAUCES). Leftovers, if you have any, make terrific sandwiches!

smelt

Broiled Fillet of Turbot

2 lbs. frozen turbot fillets, slightly thawed
4 Tblsp. butter
2 Tblsp. lemon juice

1 tsp. seafood seasoning
1 tsp. parsley flakes

Leave turbot fillets partially frozen to avoid losing moisture. Place on broiler pan rack. Dot with butter; sprinkle with lemon juice, seafood seasoning and parsley flakes. Broil for 5-7 minutes (more or less, depending on the thickness of the fillets). Turn fillets carefully with spatula only if thickness requires additional cooking time. Place on individual serving plates and serve immediately. Serves 4.

Creamed Lobster and Clams

2 green onions, sliced
3 Tblsp. butter
3 Tblsp. flour
½ tsp. salt
⅛ tsp. cayenne
1½ cups half and half
3 Tblsp. dry white wine

½ cup cooked clams, minced
½ cup cooked lobster, chopped
1 4½ oz. can button mushrooms, drained
pastry shells

In saucepan sauté onion in butter 'til tender. Blend in flour, salt and cayenne. Add half and half all at once; cook, stirring constantly, 'til mixture is thick and bubbly. Add wine, clams, lobster and mushrooms. Heat through. Serve in warm pastry shells. Serves 6.

Seafood Fettuccine

4 Tblsp. butter
3 Tblsp. onion, minced
¼ lb. fresh mushrooms, sliced
¼ cup green pepper, diced
¼ cup sweet red pepper, diced
4 Tblsp. butter
4 Tblsp. flour
1½ cups half and half

1 cup chicken broth
¼ cup grated Parmesan cheese
½ tsp. sweet basil
½ tsp. dry mustard
dash cayenne
½ tsp. seafood seasoning
½ lb. small scallops
¼ lb. crab legs or meat
fettuccine noodles

Melt 4 Tblsp. butter in saucepan. Add onion, mushrooms, green pepper and sweet red pepper. Sauté for 5 minutes; set aside. Melt remaining 4 Tblsp. butter in large skillet. Add flour and blend 'til smooth. Gradually add half and half and chicken broth stirring constantly until thickened, smooth and creamy. Stir in Parmesan cheese, sweet basil, dry mustard, cayenne, seafood seasoning, scallops and crab legs. Simmer 5-7 minutes. If sauce becomes too thick, add more chicken broth. Serve over fettuccine noodles. Excellent accompanied by a tossed green salad and sourdough rolls. Serves 4.

Cheesy Garlic Bread

1 loaf French bread,
  unsliced
½ cup butter or
  margarine

2 cloves fresh garlic,
  crushed
Parmesan cheese

Quarter French bread lengthwise. Melt butter in small saucepan and add crushed garlic. Simmer very gently until butter takes on a good, rich garlic flavor. Brush on quartered French bread. Sprinkle each quarter generously with grated Parmesan cheese. Put loaf back together, wrap in foil and place in pre-heated 425°F. oven for 15 minutes or until heated through. Remove and slice for miniature toast points. Delicious with broiled clams and oysters or as an added touch to any seafood menu.

Sauces

Cheese Sauce

2 Tblsp. butter
2 Tblsp. flour
½ cup milk
½ cup light cream
¼ cup grated Parmesan

¼ cup grated Swiss
1 egg yolk, slightly
   beaten
2 Tblsp. butter
salt and pepper

In small saucepan, melt butter and stir in flour. Blend well over low heat and stir in milk and cream. Add grated cheese, stirring constantly until smooth and creamy. Just before serving, add egg yolk and butter. Season with salt and pepper to taste. makes about 1½ cups.

Tartar Sauce

1 cup mayonnaise
¼ cup dill pickle,
   chopped fine
3 Tblsp. minced onion
2 Tblsp. lemon juice,
   vinegar or pickle juice

1 Tblsp. sugar
1 Tblsp. parsley
   flakes
salt and pepper
   to taste

Blend all ingredients thoroughly and chill. makes about 1½ cups.

Milton's Salmon Barbecue Sauce

1½ cubes butter or margarine
2 Tblsp. soy sauce
2 Tblsp. Worcestershire
½ cup brown sugar
½ tsp. garlic salt
2 Tblsp. sweet and sour sauce
dash Liquid Smoke
dash lemon juice

Combine all ingredients in saucepan and simmer over low heat. Stir constantly until mixture begins to boil. Remove from heat. Baste salmon steaks or fillets over medium-hot coals. Baste frequently. An incredible blend of flavors for an outrageous, mouth-watering treat.

Tangy Tartar

3 Tblsp. mayonnaise
4 Tblsp. plain yogurt
1 tsp. dill weed (ground)
1 tsp. onion powder
2 Tblsp. green stuffed olives, chopped fine

Combine all ingredients in small bowl and refrigerate at least one hour. Serve with your favorite fish fillets or steaks.

Cucumber Sauce

1 cup chopped cucumber
½ cup water
2 Tblsp. butter
2 Tblsp. flour
1 cup fish stock

2 Tblsp. lemon juice
1 tsp. grated lemon
   rind
½ tsp. grated onion
½ tsp. salt

Cook cucumber in water until tender. Drain. Melt butter in saucepan. Add flour and stir until blended. Slowly add fish stock. Stir over medium heat until thick and smooth. Add lemon juice, lemon rind, onion and salt, stirring constantly. Add cucumber last. Makes 2 cups.

Cocktail Sauce

1 Tblsp. grated horseradish
½ cup chili sauce
6 Tblsp. lemon juice

¼ cup catsup
5 drops tabasco
¼ tsp. celery salt

Blend all ingredients and chill at least 1 hour. Serve over crabmeat, shrimp, lobster or flaked white fish in cocktail glasses. Wonderful over steaming oysters or clams on the half shell, too!

Sauce Allemande

4 Tblsp. butter
3 Tblsp. flour
1 Tblsp. lemon juice
2 cups strong white
   fish stock

2 egg yolks
salt and pepper
   to taste

Melt butter in sauce pan; stir in flour. Bring fish stock to a boil in a seperate pan; add to butter and flour. Stir over medium heat until smooth. Beat the egg yolks and add a little of the sauce to them. Add the egg yolks to the remaining sauce, stirring constantly, keeping it below the boiling point. Season to taste.

Drawn Butter

½ cup butter
4 Tblsp. flour
½ tsp. salt

1⅔ cups hot water
¼ tsp. pepper

Melt ¼ cup of the butter. Add flour mixed with the seasonings, stirring constantly. Gradually add hot water; continue to stir. Boil 5 minutes and add remaining butter piece by piece.

Oyster Sauce

1 10-oz. jar fresh oysters
½ cup chicken broth
3 Tblsp. butter
¼ cup flour
½ cup cream
2 egg yolks, slightly
   beaten

½ Tblsp. vinegar
1 Tblsp. lemon juice
1 Tblsp. horseradish
salt and pepper,
   to taste

Parboil oysters 3-5 minutes. Drain, reserving ½ cup nectar. Allow oysters to cool slightly and chop into pieces. Add chicken broth to nectar. Melt butter and blend in flour. Whisk in cream slowly. Add oyster liquid and bring to the boiling point. Add the chopped oysters. Stir in remaining ingredients. Makes about 2 cups.

Horseradish Cream

Beat 1 cup heavy cream until stiff. Fold in 1 Tblsp. horseradish and ½ tsp. salt. Makes about 1½ cups.

Creole Sauce

1½ cups stewed tomatoes
1 green pepper, sliced
   thin
1 medium onion,
   sliced thin
¾ cup mushrooms,
   sliced
1 clove garlic, crushed

1 Tblsp. butter
1 Tblsp. flour
1 beef bouillon
   cube
½ cup hot water

Combine first 5 ingredients in a saucepan and simmer for about 10 minutes. On a separate saucepan, melt butter; add flour. Blend 'til smooth. Dissolve bouillon cube in hot water. Gradually stir into flour and butter. When thoroughly blended, add to first mixture. Cook about 5 minutes longer.

Lemon Butter

½ cup butter, softened
1 Tblsp. lemon juice

½ tsp. grated
   lemon rind

Whip butter on medium speed of electric mixer. Slowly add lemon juice and grated rind. Makes ½ cup.

Convenient Mushroom Sauce

3 Tblsp. butter
1/3 cup onions, chopped
1 clove garlic, minced
1 can condensed cream
  of mushroom soup
  (undiluted)

1 cup milk
1/4 tsp. fresh thyme
1/4 tsp. salt

In saucepan, sauté onions and garlic in butter until onions are tender and slightly transparent. Gradually whisk in undiluted mushroom soup, then milk. Add seasonings while stirring. Stir until thoroughly heated. Serve with broiled, baked or fried fish. Garnish with parsley and lemon wedges.

Lemon Dill Mayonnaise

To 1½ cups mayonnaise, add ¾ tsp. dill weed and 2 tsp. grated lemon rind. Cover and refrigerate to allow flavors to blend. Delicious with grilled salmon steaks.

Lemon Sauce

To 2 cups white cream sauce add 5 tablespoons lemon juice, 1 teaspoon grated lemon rind and ½ tsp. dry mustard. Blend well and heat through. Garnish with fresh parsley sprigs.

Egg Sauce

¼ cup butter
1½ Tblsp. flour
¾ tsp. dry mustard
¼ tsp. salt
1 Tblsp. chopped parsley

⅛ tsp. black pepper
1¼ cups milk
2 hard-cooked eggs, chopped

Melt butter in small saucepan. Stir in flour and seasonings. Gradually add milk, stirring until thick and smooth. Add eggs and parsley. Heat through. Makes 1½ cups sauce. Nice served with poached or steamed fish.

Remoulade Sauce

½ cup salad oil
¼ cup white wine
   vinegar
2 Tblsp. Dijon mustard
2 Tblsp. prepared
   horseradish
2 Tblsp. catsup
⅓ cup green onion,
   chopped fine
⅓ cup celery,
   chopped fine

¼ cup sweet red
   bell pepper,
   chopped fine
¼ tsp. salt
⅛ tsp. cayenne
1 hard-cooked egg,
   chopped
1 Tblsp. fresh snipped
   parsley

Combine all of the above ingredients.
Serve with your favorite fish fillets or
steaks. Makes about 1¾ cups.

Mornay Sauce

3 Tblsp. butter
3 Tblsp. flour
½ cup chicken broth
1 cup half-and-half
dash of cayenne

⅛ cup Parmesan
⅛ cup Swiss
1 egg yolk
2 Tblsp. butter
salt and pepper

Grate cheese and set aside. In heavy sauce pan, melt butter and stir in flour. Cook over low heat, stirring constantly, until mixture is smooth and bubbly. Stir in broth, half-and-half and cayenne. Heat to boiling, stirring constantly. Boil and stir 1 minute. Stir in cheese until melted. Just before serving, stir in slightly beaten egg yolk and 2 Tblsp. butter. Season with salt and pepper to taste. Makes about 1¾ cups.

Cindy Lou's Salmon Marinade

2 cups soy sauce
1 cup brown sugar
½ tsp. dry mustard
2 cloves garlic, minced

½ tsp. ground ginger
½ cup orange juice
concentrate

Combine all ingredients. Pierce salmon steaks or fillets. Cover with marinade. For maximum flavor, marinate a full 24 hours. Broil 10-15 minutes, depending on the size and thickness of the cuts. Delicious!

Index

A

B

C

Codfish Balls   89
Codfish Salad   91
Convenient Mushroom Sauce   139
Cooked Oyster Cocktail   47
Crab Cakes with Mornay Sauce   19
Crab Custard   17
Crab Cutlets   24
Crab Quiche   23
Crab Roll-ups   18
Crab Stuffed Scampi   20
Crab Thermidor   21
Creamed Lobster and Clams   130
Creole Sauce   138
Crisp~Coated Abalone   124
Cucumber Sauce   135
Curried Sole Fillets   114

D

Dad's Oyster Stew   49
Deborah's Smoked Salmon Dip   108
Deep Fried Halibut Cheeks   95
Deep Fried Oysters   48
Deep Fried Scallops   71
Deviled Tuna   118
Drawn Butter   136

E

Egg Sauce   140

S